Spoofing and Proofing the Classics

Literature-Based Activities to Develop Critical Reading Skills and Grammatical Knowledge

KEITH POLETTE AND NANCY POLETTE

D1569763

Teacher Ideas Press

An imprint of Libraries Unlimited

Westport, Connecticut • London

Library of Congress Cataloging-in-Publication Data

Polette, Keith, 1954-
    Spoofing and proofing the classics : literature-based activities to develop critical reading skills and grammatical knowledge / Keith Polette and Nancy Polette.
        p. cm.
    Includes bibliographical references and index.
    ISBN-13: 978-1-59158-518-3 (alk. paper)
    ISBN-10: 1-59158-518-X (alk. paper)
    1. Reading comprehension. 2. Critical thinking. 3. Children's literature, American—Study and teaching (Elementary) 4. Education, Elementary—Activity programs. I. Polette, Nancy. II. Title.
LB1573.P645 2007
372.47—dc22   2006032383

British Library Cataloguing in Publication Data is available.

Library of Congress Catalog Card Number: 2006032383
ISBN: 978-1-59158-518-3

First published in 2007

Libraries Unlimited/Teacher Ideas Press, 88 Post Road West, Westport, CT 06881
A Member of the Greenwood Publishing Group, Inc.
www.lu.com

Printed in the United States of America

The paper used in this book complies with the Permanent Paper Standard issued by the National Information Standards Organization (Z39.48–1984).

10 9 8 7 6 5 4 3 2 1

CONTENTS

INTRODUCTION

Spoofing and Proofing the Classics is designed to give young readers and writers happy, fun, and successful ways to develop critical reading (i.e., proofreading) skills and to learn some of the essential elements of grammar and usage.

We all know that editing/proofreading is an essential element of the writing process. For if a writer shares a manuscript that is riddled with mechanical and usage errors, he or she will discover that the text will not be well-received—or understood—by various audiences. The reception of such a text is hampered by errors for this simple reason: mechanical and usage errors greatly interfere with a reader's ability to process and understand the text. Think of mechanical and usage errors as the auditory and visual equivalents of "static" and "snow" on a television set: the higher the levels of static and snow, the lower the ability of the viewer to see and understand the television program. In other words, errors in a piece of writing cause communication blackouts.

One way to help young readers and writers to see how errors hamper communication is to teach them how to proofread, that is, how to develop critical reading skills. Critical reading is a selective activity (the critical reader uses few clues, not many, to make sense of the text); it is based on the reader's schema; and it is grounded in the reader's ability to know exactly what to look for during reading.

Spoofing and Proofing the Classics provides young readers and writers with a collection of "Shaggy Dog" stories, stories that are based on classic literature, but are silly and funny reworkings and extensions of them. (A "Shaggy Dog" story is an extended joke that ends with a punch-line that often takes the form of a pun or word-play).

As young readers and writers peruse these stories, they will quickly come to know what to expect, what to look for, as they read: 1) each story tells students what kinds of usage errors to scout for; and 2) each story has the same narrative structure (initial scene, introduction of setting and characters, problem/complication/conflict, resolution in the form of pun or word-play).

One reason why there are so many "Shaggy Dog" stories in our book is because proofreading skills take time, patience, and practice to develop and master. Moreover, once young readers and writers have worked through all the stories in the book, they then should be ready to turn, with a critical eye, to the texts they have written and to patrol them, that is, to be on the lookout for errors that will inhibit communication.

The ultimate aim of the book, then, is to provide young readers and writers with activities and experiences that will turn them from unknowledgeable, inexperienced proofreaders to knowledgeable, experienced ones. For only through conscious knowledge and experience can young readers sharpen their skills and can young writers craft texts that are flawless—or nearly so.

—*K. P.*

A WOLF IN SHEEP'S CLOTHING

Words the Spell-Check Won't Catch

In the following story are incorrect words the computer won't catch. Can you find them?

A certain wolf, being very hungry, spied a large flock of lambs and yewes. A shepherd aloud them to frolic in the nearly bear meadow to find awl the food they could. The shepherd was not very good at his job for he often went to sleep on chili mornings.

The best grass was found along the boarder where a wolf weighted. Hearing the shepherd's loud snore, the wolf crept on the flock and made a low rumble in his throat. The whole flock quickly disbursed and ran for safety. One ewe ran too slowly. That was the one he caught by the feat and killed, then covered himself with it's skin, and joined the flock. Day after day the idol wolf killed and ate sheep. Day after day he would caste his eyes on a victim, watch the startled ewes turn and run, then catch the slowest one for his dinner.

One night the hungry shepherd decided to kill one of the ewes for food. He looked all around to be sure his master would not catch him as he chaste a sheep. Each time he tried to get hold of a sheep it darted aweigh in a straight line. The wolf in sheep's clothing was asleep and therefore easy to catch. The crafty wolf, thinking he was about to dye, looked the shepherd in the eye and offered a bargain.

"Shepherd, my meet is old and tough. You need a tender lamb for your dinner. If you will set me free I can show you how to make a ewe turn without getting caught."

A WOLF IN SHEEP'S CLOTHING

Words the Spell-Check Won't Catch: Corrections

A certain wolf, being very hungry, spied a large flock of lambs and ewes. A shepherd **allowed** them to frolic in the nearly **bare** meadow to find **all** the food they could. The shepherd was not very good at his job for he often went to sleep on **chilly** mornings.

The best grass was found along the **border** where a wolf **waited**. Hearing the shepherd's loud snore, the wolf crept on the flock and made a low rumble in his throat. The whole flock quickly **dispersed** and ran for safety. One ewe ran too slowly. That was the one he caught by the **feet** and killed, then covered himself with it's skin, and joined the flock. Day after day the **idle** wolf killed and ate sheep. Day after day he would **cast** his eyes on a victim, watch the startled ewes turn and run, then catch the slowest one for his dinner.

One night the hungry shepherd decided to kill one of the ewes for food. He looked all around to be sure his master would not catch him as he **chased** a sheep. Each time he tried to get hold of a sheep it darted **away** in a straight line. The wolf in sheep's clothing was sleeping and therefore easy to catch. The crafty wolf, thinking he was about to **die**, looked the shepherd in the eye and offered a bargain.

"Shepherd, my **meat** is old and tough. You need a tender lamb for your dinner. If you will set me free I can show you how to make a ewe turn without getting caught."

See page 91.

A KING ARTHUR TALE

Confusing Words

In the following story are words that often are confusing: they sound similar to other words, but, when used, are incorrect. Can you find them?

Young Griflet was both pleased and surprised when King Arthur made him a knight. "There is one condition," the King told Griflet, " It is my commend that when you have undertaken your first joust, you will return to me, whether on foot or horseback."

Sir Griflet excepted the condition. Accompanied by Scrimshaw, his squire, he rode away confidentially with a great spear in his hand to challenge the first knight he met. Sure enough along came a huge knight with a shield of many colors and an even larger spear in his hand.

"I will joust with you," challenged Sir Griflet.

"It were better you did not," answered the knight, " for you are young and your might is nothing compared to mine. However, if you insist we will precede."

Sir Griflet was not to be dissuaded though it appeared his defeat was eminent. Within a split second the knight smote Sir Griflet through the shield and the truncheon stuck in his horse's body and both Sir Grifllet and his horse fell down dead.

"Oh dear, oh dear," moaned Scrimshaw. "Sir Griflet promised to return to King Arthur and appraise him of his first joust. It is up to me to see that the promise is kept even though it is his body I must return. But alas, the horse is also slain. How shall I precede? Transporting his body will be quiet a task."

A peasant who had viewed the joust from a distance spoke up. "I have a very large dog. You can have him for a piece of gold and convey your master to Camelot across the dog's back. You will surely reach there before the night is over."

Scrimshaw disproved of the old mangy dog and the greedy peasant. "I will carry my master myself," he said. "I wouldn't take a knight out on a dog like this."

A KING ARTHUR TALE

Confusing Words: Corrections

Young Griflet was both pleased and surprised when King Arthur made him a knight. "There is one condition," the King told Griflet, "It is my **command** that when you have undertaken your first joust, you will return to me, whether on foot or horseback."

Sir Griflet **accepted** the condition. Accompanied by Scrimshaw, his squire, he rode away **confidently** with a great spear in his hand to challenge the first knight he met. Sure enough along came a huge knight with a shield of many colors and an even larger spear in his hand.

"I will joust with you," challenged Sir Griflet.

"It were better you did not," answered the knight, " for you are young and your might is nothing compared to mine. However, if you insist we will **proceed**."

Sir Griflet was not to be dissuaded though it appeared his defeat was **imminent**. Within a split second the knight smote Sir Griflet through the shield and the truncheon stuck in his horse's body and both Sir Grifllet and his horse fell down dead.

"Oh dear, oh dear," moaned Scrimshaw. "Sir Griflet promised to return to King Arthur and **apprise** him of his first joust. It is up to me to see that the promise is kept even though it is his body I must return. But alas, the horse is also slain. How shall I **proceed**? Transporting his body will be **quite** a task."

A peasant who had viewed the joust from a distance spoke up. "I have a very large dog. You can have him for a piece of gold and convey your master to Camelot across the dog's back. You will surely reach there before the night is over."

Scrimshaw **disapproved** of the old mangy dog and the greedy peasant. "I will carry my master myself," he said. "I wouldn't take a knight out on a dog like this."

See page 92.

MERLIN SAVES THE DAY

More Confusing Words

In the following story are words that often are confusing: they sound similar to other words, but, when used, are incorrect. Can you find them?

When Arthur was only a baby, Merlin knew it would be no use to proclaim him as king. In resent times powerful nobles in England were veracious enough to attempt to get the kingdom for themselves, and perhaps they would kill the little prince. It was a prefect time for a battle.

Surveying the aria from the top of his castle wall, Merlin saw thorough the distance, an approaching army. A mighty lord had gathered his forces, confidant of victory. Word had spread that Merlin, the magician, had hidden the young king away. There was no way Merlin's small staff of knights could defeat or even discomfort the approaching army. Within a day the invaders would start their decent from the hill where they were camped.

"Bring me a large wood block and hides," Merlin commended his servants. From the wooden block Merlin carved the outline of a mean and fierce knight. He disbursed blackberry juice over the print and stamped the knightly image on hide after hide. The images were printed, cut out and mounted on poles above the castle walls. "We shall call our defending knight, Sir Kit!" Merlin shouted.

The approaching army neared, hoping Merlin would except surrender terms. Shields gleamed in the sun. Suddenly the steeds were brought to a halt. A bazaar sight greeted the invaders. Hundreds of fierce, mean-looking knights, armed for battle, lined the the castle walls. With cries of terror the invaders turned to dessert in full retreat never to return, all because of Merlin, the creator of the Printed Sir Kit.

MERLIN SAVES THE DAY

More Confusing Words: Corrections

When Arthur was only a baby, Merlin knew it would be no use to proclaim him as king. In **recent** times powerful nobles in England were **voracious** enough to attempt to get the kingdom for themselves, and perhaps they would kill the little prince. It was a **perfect** time for a battle.

Surveying the **area** from the top of his castle wall, Merlin saw **through** the distance, an approaching army. A mighty lord had gathered his forces, **confident** of victory. Word had spread that Merlin, the magician, had hidden the young king away. There was no way Merlin's small staff of knights could defeat or even **discomfit** the approaching army. Within a day the invaders would start their **descent** from the hill where they were camped.

"Bring me a large wood block and hides," Merlin **commanded** his servants. From the wooden block Merlin carved the outline of a mean and fierce knight. He **dispersed** blackberry juice over the print and stamped the knightly image on hide after hide. The images were printed, cut out and mounted on poles above the castle walls. "We shall call our defending knight, Sir Kit!" Merlin shouted.

The approaching army neared, hoping Merlin would **accept** surrender terms. Shields gleamed in the sun. Suddenly the steeds were brought to a halt. A **bizarre** sight greeted the invaders. Hundreds of fierce, mean-looking knights, armed for battle, lined the the castle walls. With cries of terror the invaders turned to **desert** in full retreat never to return, all because of Merlin, the creator of the Printed Sir Kit.

See page 92.

RAPUNZEL

Homophones

In the following story homophones are used incorrectly. Can you find them?

In punishment for stealing a flour from her garden, a witch took a beautiful child away from her parents. The girl was shut up in a tower, in the mist of a would, and the tower had neither steps nor door, only a small window above. When the witch wished to be let in, she would stand below and would cry, "Deer Rapunzel, let down your hare."

Rapunzel's long hare shone like gold. When she herd the voice of the witch she unbound the plates of her hair, and let it fall down lose. The witch would then climb up by it.

Alone in the tower four much of the time, Rapunzel begged the witch for a companion. The witch was not entirely evil and granted the girl's wish. She brought Rapunzel a fluffy white bunny rabbit who would scamper about the tower and cause the girl to laugh at its antics.

As time past the bunny rabbit became board with its confinement and one day surprised Rapunzel by chewing the ends of her hare.

"Stop that, you bad rabbit," Rapunzel cried and she gave the rabbit a swat that sent it flying across the tower. The rabbit retaliated by jumping on Rapunzel's lap and biting her finger.

Her cries were herd by a prince who was riding along the rode. A day earlier he had seen Rapunzel let down her hare for the witch and had come back to take his chances. "Deer Rapunzel," he called, "Let down your hare."

Rapunzel opened the window wide and leaned out. "Come back tomorrow, sweet prince," she said, "for today I am having a bad hare day."

RAPUNZEL

Homophones: Corrections

In punishment for stealing a **flower** from her garden, a witch took a beautiful child away from her parents. The girl was shut up in a tower, in the **midst** of a **wood**, and the tower had neither steps nor door, only a small window above. When the witch wished to be let in, she would stand below and would cry, "**Dear** Rapunzel, let down your hair."

Rapunzel's long **hair** shone like gold. When she herd the voice of the witch she unbound the **plaits** of her hair, and let it fall down **loose**. The witch would then climb up by it.

Alone in the tower **for** much of the time, Rapunzel begged the witch for a companion. The witch was not entirely evil and granted the girl's wish. She brought Rapunzel a fluffy white bunny rabbit who would scamper about the tower and cause the girl to laugh at its antics.

As time **passed** the bunny rabbit became **bored** with its confinement and one day surprised Rapunzel by chewing the ends of her hair.

"Stop that, you bad rabbit," Rapunzel cried and she gave the rabbit a swat that sent it flying across the tower. The rabbit retaliated by jumping on Rapunzel's lap and biting her finger.

Her cries were **heard** by a prince who was riding along the **road**. A day earlier he had seen Rapunzel let down her **hair** for the witch and had come back to take his chances. "**Dear** Rapunzel," he called, "Let down your hair."

Rapunzel opened the window wide and leaned out. "Come back tomorrow, sweet prince," she said, "for today I am having a bad hare day."

See page 93.

THE GINGERBREAD HOUSE

More Homophones

In the following story are words that often are confusing: they sound similar to other words, but, when used, are incorrect. Can you find them?

It was the third morning since Hansel and Gretel had been band from their father's house. At noon they saw a beautiful snow-white bird that flew ahead of them. They followed the bird until they came to a little house. What a cite it was! The house was made of gingerbread. The roof was made of cake and the windows were made of transparent sugar candy. The bases of the house was bred.

Little did the children know that the house was bate. Unsuspecting children would be lured by the delicious things to eat. When the hostel witch who lived there found a child eating part of the house, she invited the child inside to rest, then brood her evil spells.

The unsuspecting child was then put under a spell by the witch. Never again would the lost child return home, but would become a slave, live in a bared cage, and give the witch whatever assistants she required.

Hansel and Gretel found the gingerbread house was too delicious to resist. Hansel, the boulder child, reached up and broke off a little of the roof to see how it tasted. Gretel went up to the windowpane and nibbled at it.

At once the door opened and a woman as old as the hills came creeping out. Hansel and Gretel were so frightened that they dropped what they had in their hands. But the old woman smiled and spoke allowed.

"Dear children, come right in. I have bettor food inside. No harm will befall you. You must be tired. Come in and sit for a spell."

Good Reading: *Hansel and Gretel* by The Brothers Grimm

THE GINGERBREAD HOUSE

More Homophones: Corrections

It was the third morning since Hansel and Gretel had been **banned** from their father's house. At noon they saw a beautiful snow-white bird that flew ahead of them. They followed the bird until they came to a little house. What a **cite** it was! The house was made of gingerbread. The roof was made of cake and the windows were made of transparent sugar candy. The **basis** of the house was **bread**.

Little did the children know that the house was **bait**. Unsuspecting children would be lured by the delicious things to eat. When the **hostile** witch who lived there found a child eating part of the house, she invited the child inside to rest, then **brewed** her evil spells.

The unsuspecting child was then put under a spell by the witch. Never again would the lost child return home, but would become a slave, live in a **barred** cage, and give the witch whatever **assistance** she required.

Hansel and Gretel found the gingerbread house was too delicious to resist. Hansel, the **bolder** child, reached up and broke off a little of the roof to see how it tasted. Gretel went up to the windowpane and nibbled at it.

At once the door opened and a woman as old as the hills came creeping out. Hansel and Gretel were so frightened that they dropped what they had in their hands. But the old woman smiled and spoke **aloud**.

"Dear children, come right in. I have **better** food inside. No harm will befall you. You must be tired. Come in and sit for a spell."

See page 93.

THE BURIED TREASURE CHEST

Filler Words

Can you find and delete "filler words"? (Filler words are words that people often use when they speak but not often when they write.)

Long John Silver, like, you know, the pirate, after hours of digging finally unearthed what he had spent life looking for: the treasure chest of like Oscar the Greedy, the "Scourge of the Sea," and like the most feared pirate ever to sail the Atlantic Ocean. Grunting and groaning, sweating and straining, and tugging and pulling, Silver managed to drag Oscar's long-buried treasure chest out from the place where it had spent the last 100 years. After his labors, Silver was so exhausted.

"Arrrg!" Silver goes, "now I've like found yee! With Oscar's long buried treasure I can so give up the pirate life forever. I can finally like follow my dreams."

For the next three months no one knew where Long John Silver had gone. No one had seen him; no one had heard from him. There were, like, plenty of rumors. Some people said that Silver took the treasure and sailed south toward Argentina where he learned to dance the tango. Others, you know, said that Silver sailed to the south of Europe where he had so founded his own Pirate School. Others, though, said that Silver had like a complete makeover and was now working as a piano player on a steamboat that churned up and down the Mississippi River. And others simply shook their heads and muttered, "Long John Silver's so a'mouldering in the grave."

When the local paper hit the stands the next month, it caused quite a stir. On the second page was a large advertisement that goes:

GRAND OPENING!
Long John Silver's Rabbit Farm and Petting Zoo
Fun for the Whole Family
See the Rarest Rabbits Around — You'll Be So Amazed

When the crowds of curious customers arrived, they were greeted by like a treasure chest with a large statue of a rabbit fixed on top of it.

While one of Silver's former shipmates was buying his ticket, he turned to Silver and goes, "Say, like why did you put that rabbit on top of the treasure chest?"

Silver goes, "Well there's nothing better for attracting good luck than having a hare on your chest."

THE BURIED TREASURE CHEST

Filler Words: Corrections

Long John Silver, the pirate, after hours of digging finally unearthed what he had spent life looking for: the treasure chest of Oscar the Greedy, the "Scourge of the Sea," and the most feared pirate ever to sail the Atlantic Ocean. Grunting and groaning, sweating and straining, and tugging and pulling, Silver managed to drag Oscar's long-buried treasure chest out from the place where it had spent the last 100 years. After his labors, Silver was exhausted.

"Arrrg!" Silver exclaimed, "now I've found yee! With Oscar's long buried treasure I can now give up the pirate life forever. I can finally follow my dreams."

For the next three months no one knew where Long John Silver had gone. No one had seen him; no one had heard from him. There were, however, plenty of rumors. Some people said that Silver took the treasure and sailed south toward Argentina where he learned to dance the tango. Others said that Silver sailed to the south of Europe where he had founded his own Pirate School. Others, though, said that Silver had a complete makeover and was now working as a piano player on a steamboat that churned up and down the Mississippi River. And others simply shook their heads and muttered, "Long John Silver's a'mouldering in the grave."

When the local paper hit the stands the next month, it caused quite a stir. On the second page was a full page ad that read:

GRAND OPENING!

Long John Silver's Rabbit Farm and Petting Zoo

Fun for the Whole Family

See the Rarest Rabbits Around — You'll Be Amazed

When the crowds of curious customers arrived, they were greeted by a treasure chest with a large statue of a rabbit fixed on top of it.

While one of Silver's former shipmates was buying his ticket, he turned to Silver and said, "Say, why did you put that rabbit on top of your treasure chest?"

Silver replied, "Well there's nothing better than having a hare on your chest."

See page 94.

SICK SLEEPY HOLLOW

Malapropisms

The following story contains "malapropisms": words that are close to the "correct" word, but are wrong. Find and change the malapropisms.

Sleepy Hello was a smell and unassuming village. Its residents numbed no more than 34, but they were kind and fiendly. If one of them needed help of some kind, the others were shore to pitch end.

Ben van Tassel, the sixth of the van Tassel boys, planed to have a barn-praising on the coming weak end. Word of his tension sprayed through the village, and on Saturday morning, all of the presidents of Sleepy Hollow arrived on his farm ready to help. With sleeves rolled and toils ready, the villagers sat to work. In fact, it would have been a perfect day of working, eating, singing, dancing, and celebrating had not the skies opened up in a durge.

The villagers, being folk of sturdy flock, paid no attention to the downpar and kept working. And when they were finally finished, they were prod of the born they had raised. At day's end they all departed, went to their homes, and changed out of their psyched clothes.

That evening, though, all the villagers came down with terrible molds, molds marked not only by sneezes and shuffles, but by rough, raspy throats. Every time the poor residents of Sleepy Hollow talked, or tied to talk, their words sounded like oaks.

On Sunday morning, the tire village had gathered, as was their custom, in the local apple. The residents were excited because they were bean visited by that famous creature, Cotton Mather.

As the service began, Cotton Mather assumed the bullpit while the choir and the segregation sang hims. As he listed, Cotton Mather couldn't help but wench at the rough voices. When he addressed the segregation, his foist words were, "My friends, I must tell you that this is one hoarse town."

SICK SLEEPY HOLLOW

Malapropisms: Corrections

Sleepy **Hollow** was a **small** and unassuming village. Its residents **numbered** no more than 34, but they were kind and **friendly**. If one of them needed help of some kind, the others were **sure** to pitch **in**.

Ben van Tassel, the sixth of the van Tassel boys, **planned** to have a barn-**raising** on the coming **weekend**. Word of his **intention spread** through the village, and on Saturday morning, all of the **residents** of Sleepy Hollow arrived on his farm ready to help. With sleeves rolled and **tools** ready, the villagers **set** to work. In fact, it would have been a perfect day of working, eating, singing, dancing, and celebrating had not the skies opened up in a **deluge**.

The villagers, being folk of sturdy **stock**, paid no attention to the **downpour** and kept working. And when they were finally finished, they were **proud** of the **barn** they had raised. At day's end they all departed, went to their homes, and changed out of their **soaked** clothes.

That evening, though, all the villagers came down with terrible **colds**, **colds** marked not only by sneezes and **sniffles**, but by rough, raspy throats. Everytime the poor residents of Sleepy Hollow talked, or tied to talk, their words sounded like **croaks**.

On Sunday morning, the **entire** village had gathered, as was their custom, in the local **chapel**. The residents were excited because they were **being** visited by that famous **preacher**, Cotton Mather.

As the service began, Cotton Mather assumed the **pulpit** while the choir and the **congregation** sang **hymns**. As he **listened** Cotton Mather couldn't help but **wince** at the rough voices. When he addressed the **congregation**, his **first** words were, "My friends, I must tell you that this is one hoarse town."

THE GOTHIC GYM

More Malapropisms

The following story contains "malapropisms": words that are close to the "correct" word, but are wrong. Find and change the malapropisms.

Victor Frankenstein and his fitful, but shapely assistant, Igor, were earring the end of their labors. For mouths they had engaged in that girlish wok of roaming through graveyards and birthing the unliving to harvest legs and arms, ears and eyes, livers and spleens, hearts and lungs, and brains and bones.

After many months of collecting and classifying the body arts, Victor and Igor were in the final stooges of stitching them together to create a single being, one the likes of which had never been seen before.

Suddenly, though, there came a rapping at the laboratory door. Victor called out, "Hoot is it?"

A voice answered, "It is Director Mueller, open up at ounce."

"Just a miniature," replied Victor.

He and Igor quickly clanged into worthless clothes. Then he opened the door and grated the director.

The director required, "What is going on in here?"

Victor wiped his brew and said, "Oh, Igor and I are doing a little buddy building."

THE GOTHIC GYM

More Malapropisms: Corrections

Victor Frankenstein and his **faithful**, but **misshapen** assistant, Igor, were **nearing** the end of their labors. For **months** they had engaged in that **ghoulish work** of roaming through graveyards and **unearthing** the unliving to harvest legs and arms, ears and eyes, livers and spleens, hearts and lungs, and brains and bones.

After many months of collecting and classifying the body **parts**, Victor and Igor were in the final **stages** of stitching them together to create a single being, one the likes of which had never been seen before.

Suddenly, though, there came a rapping at the laboratory door. Victor called out, "**Who** is it?"

A voice answered, "It is **Inspector** Mueller, open up at **once**."

"Just a **minute**," replied Victor.

He and Igor quickly **changed** into **workout** clothes. Then he opened the door and **greeted** the **inspector**.

The **inspector inquired**, "What is going on in here?"

Victor wiped his **brow** and said, "Oh, Igor and I are doing a little **body** building."

BELLING THE CAT

Spelling Demons

In the following story are words spelled incorrectly. Can you find them?

The cassle mice perferred to gather together to discuss there bizness in the celler. What was to be done about the disastress cat who would sieze and eat the mice at will? It seemed that the cat was particularly fond of the youngest mice.

Many sugestions were debated when a young mouse spoke up. "We could avoid this tradgey if the cat wore a bell around its neck. That way we could hear even its most liesurely approach and excape before being caught."

The mice certenly thought it a novel idea. Of course, they would hear the cat approaching from quite a distance. There would be plenty of time to excape down the mouse hole before the cat apeared on the scene. The mice aplauded. They gave the young mouse pats on the back.

Amid all of the aplause and congratulations, an older, wiser mouse spoke up. He had given the mater thurough thought. "The idea appears clever on the surface, but which of you is willing to recieve the bell and hang it around the cat's neck?"

There was a tremendus silence. Mouse looked at mouse. They all shook their heads. No one wanted to volenteer to bell the cat.

Instead, for his clear thinking, the old mouse was given the No Bell Prize.

BELLING THE CAT

Spelling Demons: Corrections

The **castle** mice **preferred** to gather together to discuss **their business** in the **cellar**. What was to be done about the **disastrous** cat who would **seize** and eat the mice at will? It seemed that the cat was particularly fond of the youngest mice.

Many **suggestions** were debated when a young mouse spoke up. "We could avoid this **tragedy** if the cat wore a bell around its neck. That way we could hear even its most **leisurely** approach and **escape** before being caught."

The mice **certainly** thought it a novel idea. Of course, they would hear the cat approaching from quite a distance. There would be plenty of time to **escape** down the mouse hole before the cat **appeared** on the scene. The mice **applauded**. They gave the young mouse pats on the back.

Amid all of the **applause** and congratulations, an older, wiser mouse spoke up. He had given the **matter thorough** thought. "The idea appears clever on the surface, but which of you is willing to **receive** the bell and hang it around the cat's neck?"

There was a **tremendous** silence. Mouse looked at mouse. They all shook their heads. No one wanted to **volunteer** to bell the cat.

Instead, for his clear thinking, the old mouse was given the No Bell Prize.

See page 94.

RAT CLEARS A STREAM

More Spelling Demons

In the following story are words spelled incorrectly. Can you find them?

Rat was sitting at the edge of the brook analizing the disastres conditions he found there. What he saw was a substanal crop of weeds. Alot of weeds made swimming difficult. His calender told him that summer was weed seson and there was little he could do about it. Since early morning he had been trying to swim with his friends, the ducks, but a sucesion of weeds kept getting in the way. When the ducks stood on their heads, as ducks will, Rat would dive down and tickle their necks. Coming up quickly was a problem since the weeds slowed Rat's progres. In additon he recieved sharp nips on his nose from the unfreindly ducks. Finally the ducks implored Rat to go away and attend to his own afairs and leave them to mind theirs.

Rat attacked the weeds with a vengance. He had pulled quite a number from the brook when along came Mole.

"Won't you take me to call on Mr. Toad?" asked Mole. "I have heard so much about him and would like to make his aquaintence."

"Certainly," said Rat. "Get the boat out and we will vennture there at once. It's never the wrong time to call on Toad. He is always good-tempered and always glad to see visitors. It should be smooth manuvering with nothing to get in our way since I have spent the better part of the morning weeding a good brook."

Good Reading: *The Wind in the Willows* by Kenneth Grahame

RAT CLEARS A STREAM

More Spelling Demons: Corrections

Rat was sitting at the edge of the brook **analyzing** the **disastrous** conditions he found there. What he saw was a **substantial** crop of weeds. **A lot** of weeds made swimming difficult. His **calendar** told him that summer was weed **season** and there was little he could do about it. Since early morning he had been trying to swim with his friends, the ducks, but a **succession** of weeds kept getting in the way. When the ducks stood on their heads, as ducks will, Rat would dive down and tickle their necks. Coming up quickly was a problem since the weeds slowed Rat's **progress**. In **addition** he **received** sharp nips on his nose from the **unfriendly** ducks. Finally the ducks implored Rat to go away and attend to his own affairs and leave them to mind theirs.

Rat attacked the weeds with a **vengeance**. He had pulled quite a number from the brook when along came Mole.

"Won't you take me to call on Mr. Toad?" asked Mole. "I have heard so much about him and would like to make his **acquaintance**."

"Certainly," said Rat. "Get the boat out and we will **venture** there at once. It's never the wrong time to call on Toad. He is always good-tempered and always glad to see visitors. It should be smooth **maneuvering** with nothing to get in our way since I have spent the better part of the morning weeding a good brook."

See page 94.

DOWN THE RABBIT HOLE

More Spelling Demons

In the following story are words spelled incorrectly. Can you find them?

Alice was defenately tired of having nothing to do. She was considering making a daizy chain when she witnessed a strange ocurrance. A white rabbit with pink eyes was runing close by her.

The rabbit took a watch out of its wastecoat pocket, looked at it, and hurried on. Alice ran across the field after it. She was just in time to see the fasinating creture pop down a large rabbit-hole under the hedge at the edge of the cemetary.

Alice was not perticuler about where she went. She proceded down the rabbit hole that went strate down like a tunel for some way, and then dropped sudenly down and she found herself persuing the rabbit down a deep well.

Down, down, down. Would the fall never come to an end? "I wonder how many miles I have fallen by this time?" she said aloud. "I must be geting somewhere near the center of the earth."

At last the fall came to an end and Alice found she could brethe normally once more. She took a leesurely look around a wide passage and spotted the rabbit runing ahead as fast as he could.

"Wait! Wait for me!" Alice called out. "Stop running. Don't scurry. Be hoppy."

Good Reading: *Alice's Adventures in Wonderland* by Lewis Carroll

DOWN THE RABBIT HOLE

More Spelling Demons: Corrections

Alice was **definitely** tired of having nothing to do. She was considering making a **daisy** chain when she witnessed a strange **occurrence**. A white rabbit with pink eyes was **running** close by her.

The rabbit took a watch out of its **waistcoat** pocket, looked at it, and hurried on. Alice ran across the field after it. She was just in time to see the **fascinating creature** pop down a large rabbit-hole under the hedge at the edge of the **cemetery**.

Alice was not **particular** about where she went. She **proceeded** down the rabbit hole that went **straight** down like a **tunnel** for some way, and then dropped **suddenly** down and she found herself **pursuing** the rabbit down a deep well.

Down, down, down. Would the fall never come to an end? "I wonder how many miles I have fallen by this time?" she said aloud. "I must be **getting** somewhere near the center of the earth."

At last the fall came to an end and Alice found she could **breathe** normally once more. She took a **leisurely** look around a wide passage and spotted the rabbit running ahead as fast as he could.

"Wait! Wait for me!" Alice called out. "Don't scurry. Be hoppy."

See page 94.

THE FOX AND THE CROW

Double-Letter Words Missing One of the Double-Letters

Some words that have double-letters are missing one of the double-letters. Can you find and correct the words?

A fox saw two crows siting in a tre. Each had a piece of chese in its beak. The fox was determined to get the chese.

"Good morning, crows," said the fox. "What beautiful birds you are with your black and shiny feathers. It is a shame you have such a por voice. If the beauty of your voice matched the beauty of your feathers you could rule over al the other birds in the forest."

The crows were greatly insulted. They were determined to prove that their voices were inded lovely to listen to. They opened their beaks and began to caw as loudly as they could. The chese droped and the fox snatched it up and ran away shouting, "Don't trust flaterers."

The crows did not mind losing the chese. They had shown the fox that two could chep as lively as one.

THE FOX AND THE CROW

Double-Letter Words Missing One of the Double-Letters: Corrections

A fox saw two crows **sitting** in a **tree**. Each had a piece of **cheese** in its beak. The fox was determined to get the **cheese**.

"Good morning, crows," said the fox. "What beautiful birds you are with your black and shiny feathers. It is a shame you have such a **poor** voice. If the beauty of your voice matched the beauty of your feathers you could rule over **all** the other birds in the forest."

The crows were greatly insulted. They were determined to prove that their voices were **indeed** lovely to listen to. They opened their beaks and began to caw as loudly as they could. The **cheese dropped** and the fox snatched it up and ran away shouting, "Don't trust **flatterers**."

The crows did not mind losing the **cheese**. They had shown the fox that two could **cheep** as lively as one.

THE HARE AND THE TORTOISE

Words that Contain Double-Letters, but Shouldn't

Some words have double-letters that should not. Can you find and correct the words?

Hare was boasting too the other forrest animals that he could runn faster than any off them. Tortoise overhheard the boasting and challenged Hare to a race. Hare laughed but agreed, thinking itt a silly propossition. Of course he could beatt Tortoise. They asked the foxx to be the judge, and the race begaan. Hare was soon far ahead of Tortoise and lay down to takke a napp. "I can overtake Tortoise att any time," he said.

Unfortunately Hare oversleptt and found Tortoise crossing the finissh line. The other animals congrattulated Tortoise and askked him about his race. Tortoise recalled every birdd, every bllade of grass, and every fencepostt he had passed. The animals asked Tortoise how hee could remember soo many detaills.

"Well," said Tortoise, "I have turtle recall."

THE HARE AND THE TORTOISE

Words that Contain Double-Letters, but Shouldn't: Corrections

Hare was boasting **to** the other **forest** animals that he could **run** faster than any **of** them. Tortoise **overheard** the boasting and challenged Hare to a race. Hare laughed but agreed, thinking **it** a silly **proposition**. Of course he could **beat** Tortoise. They asked the **fox** to be the judge and the race **began**. Hare was soon far ahead of Tortoise and lay down to **take** a **nap**. "I can overtake Tortoise **at** any time," he said.

Unfortunately Hare **overslept** and found Tortoise crossing the **finish** line. The other animals **congratulated** Tortoise and **asked** him about his race. Tortoise recalled every **bird**, every **blade** of grass, and every **fencepost** he had passed. The animals asked Tortoise how **he** could remember **so** many **details**.

"Well," said Tortoise, "I have turtle recall."

THE ATTACK ON THE PIRATE SHIP

"O's" Changed to "I's"

In this story words that have the letter O have undergone a change. All the "O's" have been changed to the letter "I." Can you find and correct the words?

Near the miuth if the Pirate River, the Brig, the Jilly Riger, lay liw in the water. She was wrapped in a blanket if night. Captain Hiik trid the deck in thiught.

"Hiist the children up," he shiuted.

The wretched prisiners were dragged frim the hild ti walk the plank and be swalliwed by the sea. There seemed ni hipe fir Wendy and the biys.

It was then the pirates heard a dreadful screech and a criwing. In ti the deck dripped Peter Pan, the avenger. Peter threw iff his cliak, revealing twi large cans if dark red paint, ine in each hand. He flung the paint inti the faces if the pirates and dumped a can iver the head if Captain Hiik. Dark red paint spilled in the deck, causing the pirates ti slip and fall.

"Run, Wendy, run, biys," Peter shiuted. "Get away as fast as yiu can while Captain Hiik, the pirates, and his ship are mariined."

THE ATTACK ON THE PIRATE SHIP

"O's" Changed to "I's": Corrections

Near the **mouth of** the Pirate River, the Brig, the **Jolly Roger**, lay **low** in the water. She was wrapped in a blanket **of** night. Captain **Hook trod** the deck in **thought**.

"**Hoist** the children up," he **shouted**.

The wretched **prisoners** were dragged **from** the **hold to** walk the plank and be **swallowed** by the sea. There seemed **no hope for** Wendy and the **boys**.

It was then the pirates heard a dreadful screeching and a **crowing**. **On to** the deck **dropped** Peter Pan, the avenger. Peter threw **off** his **cloak,** revealing **two** large cans **of** dark red paint, **one** in each hand. He flung the paint **into** the faces **of** the pirates and dumped a can **over** the head **of** Captain **Hook**. Dark red paint spilled **on** the deck, causing the pirates **to** slip and fall.

"Run, Wendy, run, **boys**," Peter **shouted**. "Get away as fast as **you** can while Captain **Hook**, the pirates, and his ship are **marooned**."

MEN OF IRON

"A's" Changed to "E's"

In this story words that have the letter A have undergone a change. All the "A's" have been changed to the letter "E." Can you find and correct the words?

Myles, son of Sir John, wetched feerfully es e greet troop of horsemen ceme riding up to the cestle getes. He knew they were knights from the West led by the terrible Bleck Knight. He knew beceuse they cerried W speers, speers mede in the West of Englend. The knights who served Myles's fether cerried E speers, speers mede in the Eest of Englend. The E speers were fer superior to the W speers.

There wes e rustle, then footsteps end Myles's mother entered his chember. She wrepped him in e sheepskin thet ley et the foot of his bed end cerried him down the silent derkness of the winding steirwey. They were to be escorted elong e secret pessegewey to be out of herm's wey if the cestle were ettecked.

Outside, beyond the frozen moet, wes e group of derk figures weiting for them with horses. In the pellid moonlight Myles recognized the fece of Fether Edwerd, the Prior of St. Mery's.

"Do not be elermed," the priest told Myles. "You end your mother ere being moved es e preceution. Your fether's knights will win the bettle eesily for he wes very wise in his choice of weepons. All of your fether's knights cerry Britein E speers."

Good Reading: *Men of Iron* by Howard Pyle

MEN OF IRON

"A's" Changed to "E's": Corrections

Myles, son of Sir John, **watched fearfully as a great** troop of horsemen **came** riding up to the **castle gates**. He knew they were knights from the West led by the terrible **Black** Knight. He knew **because** they **carried** W **spears, spears made** in the West of **England**. The knights who served Myles's **father carried** E **spears, spears made** in the **East** of **England**. The E **spears** were **far** superior to the W **spears**.

There **was a** rustle, then footsteps **and** Myles's mother entered his **chamber**. She **wrapped** him in **a** sheepskin **that lay at** the foot of his bed and **carried** him down the silent **darkness** of the winding **stairway**. They were to be escorted **along a** secret **passageway** to be out of **harm's way** if the **castle** were **attacked**.

Outside, beyond the frozen **moat, was a** group of **dark** figures **waiting** for them with horses. In the **pallid** moonlight Myles recognized the **face** of **Father Edward**, the Prior of St. **Mary's**.

"Do not be **alarmed**," the priest told Myles. "You and your mother **are** being moved **as a precaution**. Your **father's** knights will win the **battle easily** for he **was** very wise in his choice of **weapons**. **All** of your **father's** knights **carry Britain** E **spears**."

TOAD SHOWS OFF HIS NEW CART

Missing Commas

Commas are missing in this story. Can you find where they belong?

Toad led his friends to see his gypsy caravan shining with newness. It was painted yellow with bright red wheels.

"There's the real life for you embodied in that shiny cart" said Toad. "The open road camps villages towns and cities I shall see them all. Here today up and off to somewhere else tomorrow. The whole changing world before me. And mind this is the finest cart ever built without any exception. Come inside and look at the arrangements. Planned them all myself I did."

Rat and Mole followed Toad up the steps then climbed into the caravan. It was indeed very compact and comfortable. There were sleeping bunks a table a cooking stove a birdcage with a bird in it pots pans jugs and kettles of every variety. In one corner stood a well used broom.

Toad reached for the broom. "When you have finished your visit I shall sweep the steps clean for a new cart deserves the best of care even if sweeping outside is a problem."

"Why is sweeping outside more of a problem than sweeping inside?" Mole asked.

"To sweep outside I have to tie these heavy rocks to my ankles" Toad replied. "For without the extra weight an eagle would swoop down and carry me off. That is why I weigh me down to sweep."

TOAD SHOWS OFF HIS NEW CART

Missing Commas: Corrections

Toad led his friends to see his gypsy caravan, shining with newness. It was painted yellow with bright red wheels.

"There's the real life for you embodied in that shiny cart," said Toad. "The open road, camps, villages, towns, and cities, I shall see them all. Here today, up and off to somewhere else tomorrow. The whole changing world before me. And mind, this is the finest cart ever built, without any exception. Come inside and look at the arrangements. Planned them all myself, I did."

Rat and Mole followed Toad up the steps, then climbed into the caravan. It was, indeed, very compact and comfortable. There were sleeping bunks, a table, a cooking stove, a birdcage with a bird in it, pots, pans, jugs, and kettles of every variety. In one corner stood a well used broom.

Toad reached for the broom. "When you have finished your visit, I shall sweep the steps clean, for a new cart deserves the best of care, even if sweeping outside is a problem."

"Why is sweeping outside more of a problem than sweeping inside?" Mole asked.

"To sweep outside I have to tie these heavy rocks to my ankles," Toad replied. "For without the extra weight, an eagle would swoop down and carry me off. That is why I weigh me down to sweep."

OF KNIGHTS AND SPEARS

More Missing Commas

Commas are missing in this story. Can you find where they belong?

Myles son of Sir John watched fearfully as a great troop of horsemen came riding up to the castle gates. He knew they were knights from the West led by the terrible Black Knight. He knew because they carried W spears spears made in the West of England. The knights who served Myles's father carried E spears spears made in the East of England. The E spears were far superior to the W spears.

There was a rustle then footsteps and Myles's mother entered his chamber. She dressed him in breeches stockings shirt and coat then wrapped him in a sheepskin that lay at the foot of his bed then carried him down the silent darkness of the winding stairway. They were to be escorted along a secret passageway out of harm's way if the castle were attacked.

Outside beyond the frozen moat was a group of dark figures waiting for them with horses. In the pallid moonlight Myles recognized the face of Father Edward the Prior of St. Mary's. "Look Mother " he said.

"Do not be alarmed" the priest told Myles. "You and your mother are being moved as a precaution. Your father's knights will win the battle easily for he was very wise in his choice of weapons. All of your father's knights carry Britain E spears."

Good Reading: *Men of Iron* by Howard Pyle

OF KNIGHTS AND SPEARS

More Missing Commas: Corrections

Myles, son of Sir John, watched fearfully as a great troop of horsemen came riding up to the castle gates. He knew they were knights from the West led by the terrible Black Knight. He knew because they carried W spears, spears made in the West of England. The knights who served Myles's father carried E spears, spears made in the East of England. The E spears were far superior to the W spears.

There was a rustle, then footsteps and Myles's mother entered his chamber. She dressed him in breeches, stockings, shirt, and coat and wrapped him in a sheepskin that lay at the foot of his bed, then carried him down the silent darkness of the winding stairway. They were to be escorted along a secret passageway out of harm's way if the castle were attacked.

Outside, beyond the frozen moat, was a group of dark figures waiting for them with horses. In the pallid moonlight, Myles recognized the face of Father Edward, the Prior of St. Mary's. "Look, Mother," he said.

"Do not be alarmed," the priest told Myles. "You and your mother are being moved as a precaution. Your father's knights will win the battle easily for he was very wise in his choice of weapons. All of your father's knights carry Britain E spears."

DOROTHY IN THE COUNTRY OF THE QUADLINGS

Missing Apostrophes

Apostrophes are missing in this story. Can you find where they belong?

The country of the Quadlings seemed rich and happy. There was field upon field of ripening grain with well paved roads and neat farms. The Quadlings themselves, who were short and fat and looked chubby and good natured, were dressed all in red.

Dorothy knocked on a farmhouse door. It was opened by the farmers wife, and when Dorothy asked for something to eat, the woman invited her to sit down to a good dinner. About that time the farmer entered complaining about his youngest son who made a mess of every task he tried.

"Be patient, dear," the wife replied. "He will soon get the hang of things; after all, hes only a rookie at a farm chores."

After eating three kinds of cake and four kinds of cookies, Dorothy and her companions took leave of the farmers family. She shook the hand of the farmer, his wife, and their youngest son, who spoke to her.

"Im sorry," Dorothy told the boy. "I didnt understand what you said."

"Dont pay him any attention," said the farmer. "Thats just the way the rookie mumbles."

DOROTHY IN THE COUNTRY OF THE QUADLINGS

Missing Apostrophes: Corrections

The country of the Quadlings seemed rich and happy. There was field upon field of ripening grain with well paved roads and neat farms. The Quadlings themselves, who were short and fat and looked chubby and good natured, were dressed all in red.

Dorothy knocked on a farmhouse door. It was opened by the **farmer's** wife, and when Dorothy asked for something to eat, the woman invited her to sit down to a good dinner. About that time the farmer entered complaining about his youngest son who made a mess of every task he tried.

"Be patient, dear," the wife replied. "He will soon get the hang of things; after all, **he's** only a rookie at a farm chores."

After eating three kinds of cake and four kinds of cookies, Dorothy and her companions took leave of the **farmer's** family. She shook the hand of the farmer, his wife, and their youngest son, who spoke to her.

"**I'm** sorry," Dorothy told the boy. "I **didn't** understand what you said."

"**Don't** pay him any attention," said the farmer. "**That's** just the way the rookie mumbles."

A WHALE OF A TALE

Punctuation

Punctuation is missing in this story. Can you make the corrections?

Once there was a whale that ate fishes He ate all the fishes in the ocean and there being no more fish the whale was very hungry He spied a mariner wearing a hat and blue suspenders sitting on a raft and swallowed him down hat raft suspenders and all Imagine the mariners surprise when he found he wasnt alone inside the whales warm dark stomach Another mariner was stomping about on one leg Having both had a proper upbringing the two introduced themselves

My name is Captain Scree said the most recent arrival My ship sank in a storm off the Coast of Africa I have been alone on a raft for three days until swallowed by the whale

I must explain about my name said the other mariner I am a twin and when our mother would call I was always the first to say Here I am My twin brother was always somewhere else Therefore Mother decided to name me HERE and to name my brother AWAY To this day we have carried those names and have done all things together until this huge whale came along

Oh this is certainly the largest whale I have ever encountered said the first mariner

This whale is pretty big Here answered But you should have seen the one that got Away

A WHALE OF A TALE

Punctuation: Corrections

Once there was a whale that ate fishes. He ate all the fishes in the ocean, and there being no more fish, the whale was very hungry. He spied a mariner wearing a hat and blue suspenders sitting on a raft, and swallowed him down hat, raft, suspenders and all. Imagine the mariner's surprise when he found he wasn't alone inside the whale's warm dark stomach. Another mariner was stomping about on one leg. Having both had a proper upbringing, the two introduced themselves.

"My name is Captain Scree," said the most recent arrival. "My ship sank in a storm off the Coast of Africa. I have been alone on a raft for three days until swallowed by the whale."

"I must explain about my name," said the other mariner. "I am a twin and when our mother would call, I was always the first to say 'Here I am.' My twin brother was always somewhere else. Therefore, Mother decided to name me HERE and to name my brother AWAY. To this day we have carried those names and have done all things together until this huge whale came along."

"Oh, Here, this is certainly the largest whale I have ever encountered," said the first mariner.

"This whale is pretty big," Here answered. "But you should have seen the one that got Away."

See pages 94 and 99–102.

THE YELLOW BRICK ROAD

More Punctuation

Some punctuation is missing in this story. Can you make the corrections?

A terrible cyclone picked up Dorothys house in Kansas and set it down very gently in a land of great beauty. She stood looking eagerly at the strange and beautiful sights then noticed three men and one woman coming toward her. All were oddly dressed. The woman spoke.

You are welcome most noble Sorceress to the land of the Munchkins. They are so grateful to you for having killed the Wicked Witch of the East and for setting them free from bondage. She pointed to two feet sticking out from under the house The feet were shod in silver shoes with pointed toes.

Dorothy looked and gave a little cry of fright.

Dont be afraid the woman said the evil witch cannot harm you now. I am Glinda the Good Witch of the North. The Munchkins wish to know what they can do to repay you for your kindness.

I am anxious to get back to my aunt and uncle for I am sure they will worry about me. Can you help me find my way? Dorothy asked.

You must go to the City of Emeralds and speak to the Wizard. The Munchkins have been mining yellow jades for years. They have paved the road with them. When youmeet the Wizard do not be afraid of him but tell your story and ask him to help you Good-bye, my dear

The Munchkins bowed low and wished Dorothy a pleasant journey as she set off on the track of all jades

Good Reading: *The Wonderful Wizard of Oz* by L. Frank Baum

THE YELLOW BRICK ROAD

More Punctuation: Corrections

A terrible cyclone picked up Dorothy's house in Kansas and set it down very gently in a land of great beauty. She stood looking eagerly at the strange and beautiful sights, then noticed three men and one woman coming toward her. All were oddly dressed. The woman spoke.

"You are welcome, most noble Sorceress, to the land of the Munchkins. They are so grateful to you for having killed the Wicked Witch of the East, and for setting them free from bondage." She pointed to two feet sticking out from under the house. The feet were shod in silver shoes with pointed toes.

Dorothy looked and gave a little cry of fright.

"Don't be afraid," the woman said. "The evil witch cannot harm you now. I am Glinda, the Good Witch of the North. The Munchkins wish to know what they can do to repay you for your kindness."

"I am anxious to get back to my aunt and uncle, for I am sure they will worry about me. Can you help me find my way?" Dorothy asked.

"You must go to the City of Emeralds and speak to the Wizard. The Munchkins have been mining yellow jades for years. They have paved the road with them. When you meet the Wizard do not be afraid of him but tell your story and ask him to help you. Good-bye, my dear."

The Munchkins bowed low and wished Dorothy a pleasant journey as she set off on the track of all jades.

See pages 95 and 99–102.

THE OLD SEA DOG

End Punctuation and Beginning Capital Letters

The end punctuation and beginning capital letters of sentences are missing in this story. Can you make the corrections?

i remember him as if it were yesterday, as he came plodding to the inn door, his sea-chest following him in a hand barrow the Captain was a heavy nut-brown man with hands ragged and scarred and a scar across one cheek he told dreadful stories about hanging, walking the plank, and surviving storms at sea he kept on staying month after month, and the money had been exhausted, and still my father never insisted on having more

one January morning the inn door opened to reveal the ugliest man I had ever seen he demanded to see the Captain at that moment the Captain entered the room and looked at the stranger as if he had seen a ghost the stranger said nothing but approached the old Captain's sea chest and drew a black spot on the top of it he shoved a note in the Captain's hand and left the note read, "we will come for you at midnight"

the note did not seem to bother the Captain, but the black spot did "the black spot," he shouted "they have given me the black spot" he grabbed my shoulder with a grip that almost made me cry out the expression on his face was one of mortal sickness his voice had weakened

"quick, Jim, bring soap and water before I leave this world, there is something I've got to get off my chest"

THE OLD SEA DOG

End Punctuation and Beginning Capital Letters: Corrections

I remember him as if it were yesterday, as he came plodding to the inn door, his sea-chest following him in a hand barrow. The Captain was a heavy nut-brown man with hands ragged and scarred and a scar across one cheek. He told dreadful stories about hanging, walking the plank, and surviving storms at sea. He kept on staying month after month, and the money had been exhausted, and still my father never insisted on having more.

One January morning the inn door opened to reveal the ugliest man I had ever seen. He demanded to see the Captain. At that moment the Captain entered the room and looked at the stranger as if he had seen a ghost. The stranger said nothing but approached the old Captain's sea chest and drew a black spot on the top of it. He shoved a note in the Captain's hand and left. The note read, "We will come for you at midnight."

The note did not seem to bother the Captain, but the black spot did. "The black spot," he shouted. "They have given me the black spot." He grabbed my shoulder with a grip that almost made me cry out. The expression on his face was one of mortal sickness. His voice had weakened.

"Quick, Jim, bring soap and water. Before I leave this world, there is something I've got to get off my chest."

See pages 99–102.

LITTLE JOHN HAS A TOOTHACHE

More End Punctuation and Beginning Capital Letters

The end punctuation and beginning capital letters of sentences are missing in this story. Can you make the corrections?

Robin Hood's men plunged into the forest once more and reached the spot where they dwelt in the depths of the woodland there they had built huts of bark and made couches of sweet rushes after a time they built great fires and roasted the does they had brought down with their arrows all feasted mightily except for Little John when asked why he would not partake of such a magnificent feast, he confessed he had a toothache

Friar Tuck, who acted as physician as well as spiritual advisor to the men, looked at the tooth and shook his head "it will have to come out," and thus saying, he wound a wire around the tooth, the long end of the wire protruding from Little John's mouth

Strangely enough he did not pull on the wire and cautioned the other men not to do so all that night Little John slept with the wire hanging from his mouth just before dawn he was brought fully awake with a terrible pain in his jaw friar Tuck had given the wire a mighty tug and out came the offending tooth

"why didn't you pull the tooth last night?" Little John asked

"i find this method works better," Friar Tuck replied "i call it my Pull It Surprise"

LITTLE JOHN HAS A TOOTHACHE

End Punctuation and Beginning Capital Letters: Corrections

Robin Hood's men plunged into the forest once more and reached the spot where they dwelt in the depths of the woodland. There they had built huts of bark and made couches of sweet rushes. After a time they built great fires and roasted the does they had brought down with their arrows. All feasted mightily except for Little John. When asked why he would not partake of such a magnificent feast, he confessed he had a toothache.

Friar Tuck, who acted as physician as well as spiritual advisor to the men, looked at the tooth and shook his head. "It will have to come out," and thus saying, he wound a wire around the tooth, the long end of the wire protruding from Little John's mouth.

Strangely enough he did not pull on the wire and cautioned the other men not to do so. All that night Little John slept with the wire hanging from his mouth. Just before dawn he was brought fully awake with a terrible pain in his jaw. Friar Tuck had given the wire a mighty tug and out came the offending tooth.

"Why didn't you pull the tooth last night?" Little John asked.

"I find this method works better," Friar Tuck replied. "I call it my Pull It Surprise!"

See pages 99–102.

LONG JOHN SILVER'S ESCAPE

Capitalization

Capital letters are missing in this story. Can you make the corrections?

surrounding skeleton island was a great field of open sea. the heavy steps of the pirate band were muffled by the sound of distant breakers and the chirp of countless insects in the brush. the buccaneers reached the spot where the treasure lay buried. the pirate band, with oaths and cries, began to leap, one after another, into the pit and to dig with their fingers.

"dig away, lads," captain silver shouted. after hours of digging only one piece of gold had been found. morgan held it up with a perfect spout of oaths. it was a two-guinea piece and passed from hand to hand among the pirate band for a quarter of a minute. the captain stood and watched from a distance.

"two guineas," roared morgan at captain silver. "so you've never bungled a thing, you wooden headed lubber. mates, i tell you now, that the Captain got to the treasure first. look at the face of him and you'll see it plastered there."

morgan raised his arm and his voice and plainly meant to lead a charge against captain silver. crack! crack! long john silver fired two barrels of a pistol into the advancing morgan who fell lifeless into the pit.

the pirate band rose up, murder in their eyes. the captain turned to flee. the men who had jumped at his every command now were out for his blood. he moved rapidly, leaping on his crutch till the muscles of his chest were fit to burst and threw himself into the last small boat heading for the ship.

it was at the precise moment his pirate band turned on him that captain silver learned a valuable lesson. never fight the band that heeds you!

Good Reading: *Treasure Island* by Robert Louis Stevenson

LONG JOHN SILVER'S ESCAPE

Capitalization: Corrections

Surrounding Skeleton Island was a great field of open sea. The heavy steps of the pirate band were muffled by the sound of distant breakers and the chirp of countless insects in the brush. The buccaneers reached the spot where the treasure lay buried. The pirate band, with oaths and cries, began to leap, one after another, into the pit and to dig with their fingers.

"Dig away, lads," Captain Silver shouted. After hours of digging, only one piece of gold had been found. Morgan held it up with a perfect spout of oaths. It was a two-guinea piece and passed from hand to hand among the pirate band for a quarter of a minute. The captain stood and watched from a distance.

"Two guineas," roared Morgan at Captain Silver. "So you've never bungled a thing, you wooden headed lubber. Mates, I tell you now, that the Captain got to the treasure first. Look at the face of him and you'll see it plastered there."

Morgan raised his arm and his voice and plainly meant to lead a charge against Captain Silver. CRACK! CRACK! Long John Silver fired two barrels of a pistol into the advancing Morgan who fell lifeless into the pit.

The pirate band rose up, murder in their eyes. Captain Silver turned to flee. The men who had jumped at his every command now were out for his blood. He moved rapidly, leaping on his crutch till the muscles of his chest were fit to burst and threw himself into the last small boat heading for the ship.

It was at the precise moment his pirate band turned on him that Captain Silver learned a valuable lesson. Never fight the band that heeds you!

See page 99.

THE FRANKENSTEIN MONSTER

Missing Periods, Questions Marks, and Beginning Captial Letters

Periods and question marks and the capital letters that begin sentences are missing in this story. Can you make the corrections?

victor Frankenstein devoted his life to the study of science, and in those studies saw again and again how things that die can live again if this was true, then why could he not create life knowing he could do this he made his way to the cemetery, opening graves and collecting the parts that he needed

one dark and stormy evening his work was finished he saw the creature's piercing eyes open he heard it take deep gasping breaths and watched its arms and legs shake the creature was a patchwork quilt of scars where various parts had been sewn together

to create the monster, Victor had gone without sleep and almost destroyed his health but in that eye-opening moment Victor could see no beauty the monster's yellow eyes stared through Victor without seeing him its massive mouth opened to emit a horrible gurgling sound

victor ran from the room and locked the door the creature's massive fist smashed through the door as if it were straw with thundering steps the monster headed for the cemetery at the edge of the cemetery was the cottage of the local parson by the light of the moon the parson saw the lone figure stumbling among the graves

"hey, there," the parson called out "i don't believe I know you are you from these parts"

THE FRANKENSTEIN MONSTER

Missing Periods, Question Marks, and Beginning Capital Letters: Corrections

Victor Frankenstein devoted his life to the study of science and in those studies saw again and again how things that die can live again. If this was true, then why could he not create life? Knowing he could do this he made his way to the cemetery, opening graves and collecting the parts that he needed.

One dark and stormy evening his work was finished. He saw the creature's piercing eyes open. He heard it take deep gasping breaths and watched its arms and legs shake. The creature was a patchwork quilt of scars where various parts had been sewn together.

To create the monster, Victor had gone without sleep and almost destroyed his health. But in that eye-opening moment Victor could see no beauty. The monster's yellow eyes stared through Victor without seeing him. Its massive mouth opened to emit a horrible gurgling sound.

Victor ran from the room and locked the door. The creature's massive fist smashed through the door as if it were straw. With thundering steps the monster headed for the cemetery. At the edge of the cemetery was the cottage of the local parson. By the light of the moon the parson saw the lone figure stumbling among the graves.

"Hey, there," the parson called out. "I don't believe I know you. Are you from these parts?"

See pages 99–102.

DR. FRANKENSTEIN FLEES

Missing Periods and Beginning Capital Letters

The end punctuation and capital letters that begin sentences are missing in this story. Can you make the corrections?

i could no longer confront the monster I had created i left it lying in its coffin on a cold slab in my dungeon workroom i secured the heavy oaken door with bars and chains hopefully this patchwork monstrocity would sleep until morning

i made my way up the stairs and reached my room i shivered with cold even though the flames from the fireplace heated the room well enough back and forth I trod across the heavy carpet trying to decide what to do finally, in exhaustion I collapsed on the bed and slept

it seemed no time until I was awake again i was dwarfed in the shadow of the monster who stood in the doorway, hands and feet jutting out from the smashed sides of the coffin the creature started forward, the boards of the coffin screeching as they scraped against the floorboards of my room

i had to stop the creature in its moving coffin long enough to flee down the stairs and out into the night i grabbed a bottle of Robitussin from my nightstand and threw it at the coffin the coffin stopped

DR. FRANKENSTEIN FLEES

Missing Periods and Beginning Capital Letters: Corrections

I could no longer confront the monster I had created. I left it lying in its coffin on a cold slab in my dungeon workroom. I secured the heavy oaken door with bars and chains. Hopefully this patchwork monstrocity would sleep until morning.

I made my way up the stairs and reached my room. I shivered with cold even though the flames from the fireplace heated the room well enough. Back and forth I trod across the heavy carpet trying to decide what to do. Finally, in exhaustion I collapsed on the bed and slept.

It seemed no time until I was awake again. I was dwarfed in the shadow of the monster who stood in the doorway, hands and feet jutting out from the smashed sides of the coffin. The creature started forward, the boards of the coffin screeching as they scraped against the floorboards of my room.

I had to stop the creature in its moving coffin long enough to flee down the stairs and out into the night. I grabbed a bottle of Robitussin from my nightstand and threw it at the coffin. The coffin stopped.

See pages 99–102.

ROBIN HOOD AND THE SHERIFF

Missing Quotation Marks

Quotation marks are missing in this story. Can you make the corrections?

An arrow shot through the forest and found its mark in Robin Hood's camp. Attached to the arrow was a torn page from Friar Tuck's prayer book. A message had been written on the prayer page:

The Sheriff of Nottingham

knows your hiding place.

Run!

Robin Hood laughed and set forth his plan to capture the sheriff. Disguised as an old beggar, he carried out his plan.

You lily-livered cowards, pretending to be what you are not, the sheriff yelled. You cannot keep me prisoner for long. My men are searching for me now.

Quiet, Sheriff, Robin Hood replied. Your temper will do you no good. Do sit down, Sir, and join us in a repast. The meal will cost you one bag of gold, a pittance that you will not miss. As for the men searching for you, we shall know when they are near.

How can you possibly know the location of my men? the sheriff asked.

The same way we knew you were coming, Robin Hood answered. Friar Tuck will send another prayer page with a message. It will be shot through the air by bow and arrow. We call it our system of guided missives.

ROBIN HOOD AND THE SHERIFF

Missing Quotation Marks: Corrections

An arrow shot through the forest and found its mark in Robin Hood's camp. Attached to the arrow was a torn page from Friar Tuck's prayer book. A message had been written on the prayer page:

The Sheriff of Nottingham

knows your hiding place.

Run!

Robin Hood laughed and set forth his plan to capture the sheriff. Disguised as an old beggar, he carried out his plan.

"You lily-livered cowards, pretending to be what you are not," the sheriff yelled. "You cannot keep me prisoner for long. My men are searching for me now."

"Quiet, Sheriff," Robin Hood replied. "Your temper will do you no good. Do sit down, Sir, and join us in a repast. The meal will cost you one bag of gold, a pittance that you will not miss. As for the men searching for you, we shall know when they are near."

"How can you possibly know the location of my men?" the sheriff asked.

"The same way we knew you were coming," Robin Hood answered. "Friar Tuck will send another prayer page with a message. It will be shot through the air by bow and arrow. We call it our system of guided missives."

See page 101.

SNOW WHITE AND THE SEVEN DWARFS

What's Wrong with the Verb?

Some verbs are incorrect (form, tense). Can you make the corrections?

The dwarfs, when they arriving home in the evening, finded Snow White lying on the ground. There camed no breath out of her mouth. They lifted her up, cut her laces, combed her hair, and washed her with water, but to no avail. She will be dead. They laying her on a bier and tooking her picture. A passing peddler took the film to have been developed. It was the custom that pictures of the deceased be display at the funeral.

Day after day passing. They maked a coffin of clear glass, so it could be looked into from all sides. They setting the coffin out upon the mountain, and one of them always remained by it to watch. Day after day they watching for the return of the peddler, for they could not have been having the funeral without the pictures. Snow White lay in the coffin looking as if she are asleep, for she was still as white as snow.

"We cannot delaying the funeral much longer," saying one of the dwarfs to the one who had took the pictures.

"Just a few more days," the other reply. "For I feel that one day soon my prints will come."

SNOW WHITE AND THE SEVEN DWARFS

What's Wrong with the Verb?: Corrections

The dwarfs, when they **arrived** home in the evening, **found** Snow White lying on the ground. There **came** no breath out of her mouth. They lifted her up, cut her laces, combed her hair, and washed her with water, but to no avail. She **was** dead. They **laid** her on a bier and **took** her picture. A passing peddler took the film **to be** developed. It was the custom that pictures of the deceased be **displayed** at the funeral.

Day after day **passed**. They **made** a coffin of clear glass, so that it could be looked into from all sides. They **set** the coffin out upon the mountain, and one of them always remained by it to watch. Day after day they **watched** for the return of the peddler, for they could not **have** the funeral without the pictures. Snow White lay in the coffin looking as if she **were** asleep, for she was still as white as snow.

"We cannot **delay** the funeral much longer," **said** one of the dwarfs to the one who had **taken** the pictures.

"Just a few more days," the other **replied**. "For I feel that one day soon my prints will come."

See pages 95–96.

ALADDIN MEETS THE GENIE

What's Wrong with the Verb?

Some verbs are incorrect (form, tense) in this story. Can you make the corrections?

When a cruel magician roll a great stone over the entrance, Aladdin find himself trap in a dark cave. For two days he remain in the dark crying and lamenting. On the third day, without thinking, he rub the ring that the magician had forget to take from him. Immediately an enormous and frightening genie rised out of the earth. In his huge hand is'd a small rabbit with soft, light brown fur.

The genie spoked. "What wouldst thou with me? I am the Slave of the Ring and will obey thee in all things."

Aladdin replied, "Delivering me from this horrible, dark cave!" whereupon the earth open and he finded himself outside. As soon as his eyes could be bear the light he goed home, but fainting on the threshold. When he come to, he showed his mother the fruits he will have gathered in the garden, which was really precious stones. He then told her of his imprisonment in the cave and asking for food.

"My child," say his mother, "how did you escaped from such a dark and dreadful place?"

"I could not have doed it alone," Aladdin replied. "My escape was made possible by this genie with the light brown hare."

ALADDIN MEETS THE GENIE

What's Wrong with the Verb?: Corrections

When a cruel magician **rolled** a great stone over the entrance, Aladdin **found** himself **trapped** in a dark cave. For two days he **remained** in the dark crying and lamenting. On the third day, without thinking, he **rubbed** the ring that the magician **had forgotten** to take from him. Immediately an enormous and frightening genie **rose** out of the earth. In his huge hand **was** a small rabbit with soft, light brown fur.

The genie spoke. "What wouldst thou with me? I am the Slave of the Ring and will obey thee in all things."

Aladdin replied, "**Deliver** me from this horrible, dark cave!" whereupon the earth **opened** and he **found** himself outside. As soon as his eyes could bear the light he **went** home, but **fainted** on the threshold. When he **came** to, he showed his mother the fruits he **had gathered** in the garden, which **were** really precious stones. He then **told** her of his imprisonment in the cave and **asked** for food.

"My child," said his mother. "How did you ever **escape** from such a dark and dreadful place?"

"I could not have **done** it alone," Aladdin replied. "My escape was made possible by this genie with the light brown hare."

See pages 95–96.

DOROTHY IN THE CHINA COUNTRY

Incorrect Pronouns

Some pronouns are incorrect in this story. Can you make the corrections?

Dorothy and his companions arrived in a country with a floor as smooth and shining as the bottom of a big platter. Scattered around were many houses made of china and painted the brightest colors. The houses were small, the biggest of they reaching only Dorothy's waist.

The people were also made of china. There were milkmaids and shepherds and clowns, and a prince and princess with jeweled crowns, both crying great tears. When Dorothy inquired as to the cause of such sorrow the prince spoke up.

"Someones has stolen our royal thrones. One cannot possibly be a proper prince or princess without a throne."

Meanwhile, Scarecrow was stepping carefully among the houses. They was peeking in their windows to see tiny china couches and tables and chairs and beds where the china people slept. Imagine us surprise when in one of the china houses they saw two thrones.

As carefully as it could, Scarecrow reached into the house to remove the thrones and restore tham to they owners. Sad to say, she was not careful enough. Just as them removed the last throne, the glass house shattered.

"Do not apologize for destroying the house," said the prince. "For people whom live in glass houses should not stow thrones."

DOROTHY IN THE CHINA COUNTRY

Incorrect Pronouns: Corrections

Dorothy and **her** companions arrived in a country with a floor as smooth and shining as the bottom of a big platter. Scattered around were many houses made of china and painted the brightest colors. The houses were small, the biggest of **them** reaching only Dorothy's waist.

The people were also made of china. There were milkmaids and shepherds and clowns and a prince and princess with jeweled crowns, both crying great tears. When Dorothy inquired as to the cause of such sorrow the prince spoke up.

"Someone has stolen our royal thrones. One cannot possibly be a proper prince or princess without a throne."

Meanwhile, Scarecrow was stepping carefully among the houses. **He** was peeking in their windows to see tiny china couches and tables and chairs and beds where the china people slept. Imagine **his** surprise when in one of the china houses **he** saw two thrones.

As carefully as **he** could, Scarecrow reached into the house to remove the thrones and restore **them** to **their** owners. Sad to say, **he** was not careful enough. Just as **he** removed the last throne, the glass house shattered.

"Do not apologize for destroying the house," said the prince. "For people **who** live in glass houses should not stow thrones."

See page 96.

AN UNHAPPY CAPTAIN SMOLLETT

What's Wrong with the Prepositions?

Some prepositions are incorrect in this story. Can you make the corrections?

Captain Smollett spoke plainly at the squire, "Sir, I don't like this cruise; I don't like the men; and I don't like First Officer Grim, that's the short and sweet on it."

"You say you don't like the crew or First Officer Grim," the squire replied. "Are they not good seamen?"

"That, sir, is between the point. I understand you're going after treasure, that you have a map in an island, that there's crosses beyond the map to show where the treasure is." He then named the latitude and longitude exactly. "When treasure is involved you need a first officer who can control the men. That means he has to be a crack shot."

"Does First Officer Grim not qualify?" asked the squire.

"I should say not," the Captain replied. "Men that I choose to sail with me must show their skill besides high scores amid a shooting contest each year. The First Officer has never sailed with me and I understand he has always had low scores and refuses to participate until any shooting contest. His last four scores were seven years ago!"

AN UNHAPPY CAPTAIN SMOLLETT

What's Wrong with the Prepositions?: Corrections

Captain Smollett spoke plainly to the squire, "Sir, I don't like this cruise; I don't like the men; and I don't like First Officer Grim, that's the short and sweet **of** it."

"You say you don't like the crew or First Officer Grim," the squire replied. "Are they not good seamen?"

"That, sir, is **beside** the point. I understand you're going after treasure, that you have a map **of** an island, that there's crosses **on** the map to show where the treasure is." He then named the latitude and longitude exactly. "When treasure is involved you need a first officer who can control the men. That means he has to be a crack shot."

"Does First Officer Grim not qualify?" asked the squire.

"I should say not," the Captain replied. "Men that I choose to sail with me must show their skill **with** high scores **in** a shooting contest each year. The First Officer has never sailed with me and I understand he has always had low scores and refuses to participate **in** any shooting contest. His last four scores were seven years ago!"

See pages 96–97.

ROBIN HOOD AT THE FAIR

Incorrect Conjunctions

Some conjunctions are incorrect in this story. Can you make the corrections?

Robin Hood as band of merry men awoke in Sherwood Forest when the birds were singing or the sun was shining. Robin spoke to his band of men, "For fourteen days we have seen no sport, so now we will go to the fair in Nottingham Town since enjoy ourselves."

The merry band made their way through highway and byway when along forest skirts after they arrived at the fair. In the crowded streets were monks and knights, shopkeepers and maidens, and sellers of all sorts of goods.

A magician had set up shop in the middle of the square or performed for the crowds. White doves flew from his hat, amazing lights danced from one hand to another. He then announced that he would perform his most spectacular trick, sawing a person in half. "I need a volunteer," he shouted.

Friar Tuck, the only brother of Robin Hood, stepped forward. The crowd grew silent as the rotund friar was placed in a box or sawed in half. Unfortunately the trick didn't work. The magician could not put the two halves back together.

In years to come when Robin Hood was questioned about his family, his reply was, "Sad to say I have only one half brother."

ROBIN HOOD AT THE FAIR

Incorrect Conjunctions: Corrections

Robin Hood **and** band of merry men awoke in Sherwood Forest when the birds were singing **and** the sun was shining. Robin spoke to his band of men, "For fourteen days we have seen no sport, so now we will go to the fair in Nottingham Town **and** enjoy ourselves."

The merry band made their way through highway and byway **and** along forest skirts **until** they arrived at the fair. In the crowded streets were monks and knights, shopkeepers and maidens, and sellers of all sorts of goods.

A magician had set up shop in the middle of the square **and** performed for the crowds. White doves flew from his hat, amazing lights danced from one hand to another. He then announced that he would perform his most spectacular trick, sawing a person in half. "I need a volunteer," he shouted.

Friar Tuck, the only brother of Robin Hood, stepped forward. The crowd grew silent as the rotund friar was placed in a box **and** sawed in half. Unfortunately the trick didn't work. The magician could not put the two halves back together.

In years to come when Robin Hood was questioned about his family, his reply was, "Sad to say I have only one half brother."

See pages 97–98.

DOROTHY AND TOTO

Sentences and Not-Sentences

This story contains groups of words that may look like sentences, but are not complete. Can you make the corrections?

Uncle Henry looked anxiously at the sky, which was even greyer than usual. The tall grass in waves before the coming storm. A sharp whistling in the air from the south.

"Get in the house, there's a cyclone coming," Uncle Henry shouted. Toward the sheds where the cows and horses were kept.

Toto out of Dorothy's arms and under the piano. The girl after him. Then, a strange thing happened. The house whirled around two or three times and then rose in the air. When Dorothy halfway across the room, a great shriek from the wind. It up the little dog and him on top of the piano. Dorothy her pet just as the strong pressure from the air allowed neither to move.

When the house was finally set down in a strange land, Dorothy the mayor of the Munchkins.

"Who you, my dear, and how you get here?" asked the mayor.

"I Dorothy Gale from Kansas," she replied. "A cyclone me here. This my dog, Toto. He accompanied me on the piano."

DOROTHY AND TOTO

Sentences and Not-Sentences: Corrections

Uncle Henry looked anxiously at the sky, which was even greyer than usual. The tall grass **bowed** in waves before the coming storm. **There now came a** sharp whistling in the air from the south.

"Get in the house, there's a cyclone coming," Uncle Henry shouted. **He ran toward** the sheds where the cows and horses were kept.

Toto **jumped** out of Dorothy's arms and **hid** under the piano. The girl **ran** after him. Then, a strange thing happened. The house whirled around two or three times and then rose in the air. When Dorothy **was** halfway across the room, **there was a** great shriek from the wind. It **lifted** up the little dog and **set** him on top of the piano. Dorothy **reached** her pet just as the strong pressure from the air allowed neither to move.

When the house was finally set down in a strange land, Dorothy **was greeted by** the mayor of the Munchkins.

"Who are you, my dear, and how did you get here?" asked the mayor.

"I **am** Dorothy Gale from Kansas," she replied. "A cyclone **blew** me here. This is my dog, Toto. He accompanied me on the piano."

See pages 103–105.

COLIN VISITS THE SECRET GARDEN

Is It a Sentence?

This story contains groups of words that may look like sentences, but are not. Can you make the corrections?

The secret garden bloomed and bloomed and every morning revealed new miracles. A robin in her nest watched. Mary as she pushed Colin's chair slowly and steadily. Past flowers of gold and purple and red and violet.

"Look at the robin's head!" Colin exclaimed. "The robin is bobbin!"

He was not at all the same boy Mary had found one night in a dark bedroom in the Manor House. Screaming and beating his pillow. "Stop that screaming at once," she shouted. "What is the matter with you?"

"I am ill," the boy cried. "If I live I may be a hunchback, but I shan't live. I have spent most of my life. In bed and I shall spend the rest of it here."

Mary knew better. As the weeks passed. Colin's health improved. Mary took him to her secret garden. Every morning revealed. New surprises most mornings they were joined by Mary's friend, Dickon. They sat under the plum tree, which was snow-white. With blossoms and musical with bees. Bits of blue sky. Looked down on the children like wonderful eyes.

"Look, look," Colin cried. "The bees are in the trees. There's a snake by the rake. The rose is in a pose."

Dickon looked puzzled. "Why is Colin speaking in rhyme?" he asked.

Mary smiled. "You might say he has gone from bed to verse."

Good Reading: *The Secret Garden* by Frances Hodgson Burnett

COLIN VISITS THE SECRET GARDEN

Is It a Sentence?: Corrections

The secret garden bloomed and bloomed and every morning revealed new miracles. A robin in her nest watched Mary as she pushed Colin's chair slowly and steadily past flowers of gold and purple and red and violet.

"Look at the robin's head!" Colin exclaimed. "The robin is bobbin!"

He was not at all the same boy Mary had found one night in a dark bedroom in the Manor House screaming and beating his pillow. "Stop that screaming at once," she shouted. "What is the matter with you?"

"I am ill," the boy cried. "If I live I may be a hunchback, but I shan't live. I have spent most of my life in bed and I shall spend the rest of it here."

Mary knew better. As the weeks passed and Colin's health improved, Mary took him to her secret garden. Every morning revealed new surprises. Most mornings they were joined by Mary's friend, Dickon. They sat under the plum tree, which was snow-white with blossoms and musical with bees. Bits of blue sky looked down on the children like wonderful eyes.

"Look, look," Colin cried. "The bees are in the trees. There's a snake by the rake. The rose is in a pose."

Dickon looked puzzled. "Why is Colin speaking in rhyme?" he asked.

Mary smiled. "You might say he has gone from bed to verse."

See pages 103–105.

TOM SAWYER PRETENDS

Is It a Sentence?

This story contains groups of words that may look like sentences, but are not. Can you make the corrections?

Tom lay thinking presently it occurred to him that he wished he was sick; then he could stay. Home from school. Here was a vague. Possibility he canvassed his system. No ailment was found, and he investigated again nothing. He could think of nothing. Then he remembered two things. Yesterday Tom and Huck had sneaked. Into the local theater to watch a mime perform. Wow, was he good! That mime could make you believe. He was anything and anybody. The second thing Tom remembered. Was the local doctor telling about a certain thing that laid a patient low. For two or three weeks and threatened to make him lose his voice.

Tom fell to thrashing. Around with considerable spirit. He wrinkled his face. And puffed out his cheeks. By the time Aunt Polly looked at the boy. He was panting with his exertions and had swelled. Himself up as big as a toad. As she stared at Tom her face grew. White and her lip trembled. Then she saw the wink Tom gave Huck. Who had climbed the steps behind her.

"Tom, stop this nonsense and climb out of bed this minute. So, all this mime was because you thought. You'd get to stay home from school," Aunt Polly yelled.

A sheepish Tom. Climbed out of bed fully dressed. It was too late for breakfast. As Tom and Huck left the house on the way to school. Throwing wide the door. Aunt Polly called after them.

"Tom, ask your teacher if you can start an acting class at school. After all, a mime is a terrible thing to waste."

TOM SAWYER PRETENDS

Is It a Sentence?: Corrections

Tom lay thinking. Presently it occurred to him that he wished he was sick, then he could stay home from school. Here was a vague possibility. He canvassed his system. No ailment was found, and he investigated again. He could think of nothing. Then he remembered two things. Yesterday Tom and Huck had sneaked into the local theater to watch a mime perform. Wow, was he good! That mime could make you believe he was anything and anybody. The second thing Tom remembered was the local doctor telling about a certain thing that laid a patient low for two or three weeks and threatened to make him lose his voice.

Tom fell to thrashing around with considerable spirit. He wrinkled his face and puffed out his cheeks. By the time Aunt Polly looked at the boy he was panting with his exertions and had swelled himself up as big as a toad. As she stared at Tom her face grew white and her lip trembled. Then she saw the wink Tom gave Huck, who had climbed the steps behind her.

"Tom, stop this nonsense and climb out of bed this minute. So, all this mime was because you thought you'd get to stay home from school," Aunt Polly yelled.

A sheepish Tom climbed out of bed fully dressed. It was too late for breakfast as Tom and Huck left the house on the way to school. Throwing wide the door, Aunt Polly called after them.

"Tom, ask your teacher if you can start an acting class at school. After all, a mime is a terrible thing to waste."

See pages 103–105.

TOM AT CHURCH

Where Do the Semicolons Belong?

This story contains independent clauses that are not connected with semicolons. Can you make the corrections?

It was time for the Sunday School superintendent to make his usual speech. The less-than-eager children were bored, they wiggled in the high-backed, uncushioned pews. The hard wood under their bottoms had a slick shine that made it ideal for sliding. Tom and Huck relieved their boredom by challenging each other to see who could slide the farthest before getting caught.

The superintendent spoke. "Now children, I want you all to sit up just as straight and pretty as you can, give me all of your attention. I want to tell you how good it makes me feel to see so many bright, clean little faces, learning to do right and to be good."

The speech went on and on, it was often interrupted by fidgetings and whisperings that extended far and wide, not to mention fights and other recreations among certain of the boys.

It was not long before the superintendent saw Tom and Huck busily engaged in their sliding contest. "Stop that sliding at once," he ordered. "There are strict rules that must be followed in church. One of them is NO SLIDING IN THE PEWS!"

Tom ignored the superintendent's words; he slid clear to the end of a pew as fast as a downhill skier. In fact, his speed was great, it was so great that he slid off the end and hit the floor with a thump.

"Young man," the superintendent called, "why are you ignoring the rule of no sliding in the pews?"

"Well, Sir," Tom drawled, "haven't you heard that in this age of wondrous inventions nobody uses a slide rule anymore."

TOM AT CHURCH

Where Do the Semicolons Belong?: Corrections

It was time for the Sunday School superintendent to make his usual speech. The less-than-eager children were bored; they wiggled in the high-backed, uncushioned pews. The hard wood under their bottoms had a slick shine that made it ideal for sliding. Tom and Huck relieved their boredom by challenging each other to see who could slide the farthest before getting caught.

The superintendent spoke. "Now children, I want you all to sit up just as straight and pretty as you can; give me all of your attention. I want to tell you how good it makes me feel to see so many bright, clean little faces, learning to do right and to be good."

The speech went on and on; it was often interrupted by fidgetings and whisperings that extended far and wide, not to mention fights and other recreations among certain of the boys.

It was not long before the superintendent saw Tom and Huck busily engaged in their sliding contest. "Stop that sliding at once," he ordered. "There are strict rules that must be followed in church. One of them is NO SLIDING IN THE PEWS!"

Tom ignored the superintendent's words; he slid clear to the end of a pew as fast as a downhill skier. In fact, his speed was great; it was so great that he slid off the end and hit the floor with a thump.

"Young man," the superintendent called, "why are you ignoring the rule of no sliding in the pews?"

"Well, Sir," Tom drawled, "haven't you heard that in this age of wondrous inventions nobody uses a slide rule anymore."

See page 101.

TOM FINDS INJUN JOE

Where Do the Semicolons Belong?

This story contains independent clauses that are not connected with semicolons. Can you make the corrections?

The cave door was unlocked, Tom and the others entered to see Injun Joe stretched along the ground, dead. Tom was touched, he knew how this wretch had suffered, alone and without friends.

Injun Joe's bowie knife lay close by, its blade was broken in two. The door had been chipped and hacked at with tremendous effort. Upon that stubborn material the knife had no impact. Injun Joe had only hacked at the door in order to pass the time. Ordinarily one could find bits of candle stuck in the crevices of the wall, there were none now. The prisoner had searched them out, he had eaten them. He had contrived to catch a few bats that he had also eaten. Water came from the drip of a stalactite overhead, it fell one drop at a time.

Tom felt sorry for Injun Joe, but at the same time he felt a sense of relief. He had not realized until now the sense of dread he had lived with since the day he lifted his voice against the Indian no one really knew.

Injun Joe was buried near the mouth of the cave, people flocked there in boats and wagons from the towns and from all the farms for seven miles around. They brought their children, they brought all sorts of provisions. They confessed they had a most satisfactory time and agreed with the words on Injun Joe's tombstone: Here Lies the Lonesome Stranger.

TOM FINDS INJUN JOE

Where Do the Semicolons Belong?: Corrections

The cave door was unlocked; Tom and the others entered to see Injun Joe stretched along the ground, dead. Tom was touched; he knew how this wretch had suffered, alone and without friends.

Injun Joe's bowie knife lay close by; its blade was broken in two. The door had been chipped and hacked at with tremendous effort. Upon that stubborn material the knife had no impact. Injun Joe had only hacked at the door in order to pass the time. Ordinarily one could find bits of candle stuck in the crevices of the wall; there were none now. The prisoner had searched them out; he had eaten them. He had contrived to catch a few bats that he had also eaten. Water came from the drip of a stalactite overhead; it fell one drop at a time.

Tom felt sorry for Injun Joe, but at the same time he felt a sense of relief. He had not realized until now the sense of dread he had lived with since the day he lifted his voice against the Indian no one really knew.

Injun Joe was buried near the mouth of the cave; people flocked there in boats and wagons from the towns and from all the farms for seven miles around. They brought their children; they brought all sorts of provisions. They confessed they had a most satisfactory time and agreed with the words on Injun Joe's tombstone: Here Lies the Lonesome Stranger.

See page 101.

SOARING HOME

Run-on Sentences

Correct the run-on sentences in the following story. Run-on sentences in this story take the form of two independent clauses that are not separated by any punctuation.

Dorothy and the Wizard of Oz climbed into the basket of his hot air balloon she threw kisses and flowers to all the residents of Oz who had arrived to bid them farewell.

The Wizard ignited the gas burner, opened the valve, and sent gusts of hot air into the balloon within minutes, the balloon expanded, grew plump, and lifted into the azure sky.

Riding the air currents, Dorothy and the Wizard drifted away from Oz they sailed over rivers and plains, forests and fields, mountains and meadows their journey had become a breeze.

The air began to change, becoming choppy the temperature dropped as they drifted toward a great grey wall of clouds.

The Wizard said, "Hold on Dorothy, it's going to be a bumpy ride!"

Dorothy replied, "Isn't there anything we can do to avoid the storm?"

"I'm afraid not," said the Wizard. "Balloons don't have steering wheels!"

As the storm hit, the balloon was buffetted it was tossed back and forth and up and down by the invisible hands of the wind then the rain saturated Dorothy and the Wizard it soaked the balloon heavy with water, the balloon slowly sank toward the ground.

"We're going to crash!" exclaimed Dorothy.

"I have an idea," cried the Wizard.

He reached into his pocket and removed a small white object that looked like a thin piece of chalk he threw it overboard immediately the balloon lifted, freed itself from the grip of the storm, and continued on its way to Kansas.

"What did you throw out?" asked Dorothy.

"My last cigarette," replied the Wizard.

"Why?" inquired Dorothy.

"Well," said the Wizard, "it was clear that we needed to make this balloon a cigarette lighter."

SOARING HOME

Run-on Sentences: Corrections

Dorothy and the Wizard of Oz climbed into the basket of his hot air balloon. She threw kisses and flowers to all the residents of Oz who had arrived to bid them farewell.

The Wizard ignited the gas burner, opened the valve, and sent gusts of hot air into the balloon. Within minutes, the balloon expanded, grew plump, and lifted into the azure sky.

Riding the air currents, Dorothy and the Wizard drifted away from Oz. They sailed over rivers and plains, forests and fields, mountains and meadows. Their journey had become a breeze.

The air began to change, becoming choppy. The temperature dropped as they drifted toward a great grey wall of clouds.

The Wizard said, "Hold on Dorothy, it's going to be a bumpy ride!"

Dorothy replied, "Isn't there anything we can do to avoid the storm?"

"I'm afraid not," said the Wizard. "Balloons don't have steering wheels!"

As the storm hit, the balloon was buffetted. It was tossed back and forth and up and down by the invisible hands of the wind. Then the rain saturated Dorothy and the Wizard; it soaked the balloon. Heavy with water, the balloon sank toward the ground.

"We're going to crash!" exclaimed Dorothy.

"I have an idea," cried the Wizard.

He reached into his pocket and removed a small white object that looked like a thin piece of chalk. He threw it overboard. Immediately the balloon lifted, freed itself from the grip of the storm, and continued on its way to Kansas.

"What did you throw out?" asked Dorothy.

"My last cigarette," replied the Wizard.

"Why?" inquired Dorothy.

"Well," said the Wizard, "it was clear that we needed to make this balloon a cigarette lighter."

See pages 99–102.

GOLD FEVER

More Run-on Sentences

Correct the run-on sentences in the following story. Run-on sentences in this story take the form of two independent clauses that are separated by commas.

Having had enough of life on the Mississippi, Huck Finn lit out for the west, he travelled for weeks until he finally stopped at Sutter's Mill where he decided to become a gold prospector, with what little money he had, he bought a patch of land, a pick and a shovel, a lamp, and a month's supply of food, then he began digging.

Day in and day out, he dug, he dug for weeks, he dug in the sun, he dug in the rain, he dug during windstorms, he dug from dawn to dusk.

Then he hit gold, gold that shimmered like the yellow eyes of a blackbird, Huck scurried to town, cashed in his gold, and bought equipment to lay a track into his mine.

Over the next few months, Huck continued to hit gold, in fact, he hit so much gold that his one car on his one track couldn't carry it all, the gold he dug began to collect in the back of the mine.

Other prospectors who'd heard about Huck's great find came by to see for themselves, they all tried to convince Huck to put more tracks in the mine, "If you do," they would say, "you can get all gold out faster, as it is, most of it is just sittin' there, deep in the mine."

Huck refused, no matter what others said to persuade him to lay more tracks, he just shook his head and walked away.

One day, a fellow by the name of Mark Twain stopped by, he too had heard about Huck's claim and wanted to satisfy his curiosity, he noticed a few other miners milling about and struck up a conversation with them.

"Seems that this fella's doin' pretty well," said Twain.

"Sure is," said the others.

"If he's doing so well," said Twain, "why doesn't he lay more tracks?"

"Mister," said one of the others, "you'll never convince him to do that."

"Why's that?" asked Twain.

"Because," replied the other, "Huck Finn's got a one track mine, and that's all there is to it."

GOLD FEVER

More Run-on Sentences: Corrections

Having had enough of life on the Mississippi, Huck Finn lit out for the west. He travelled for weeks until he finally stopped at Sutter's Mill where he decided to become a gold prospector. With what little money he had, he bought a patch of land, a pick and a shovel, a lamp, and a month's supply of food. Then he began digging.

Day in and day out, he dug. He dug for weeks. He dug in the sun, he dug in the rain, he dug during windstorms, he dug from dawn to dusk.

Then he hit gold. Gold that shimmered like the yellow eyes of a blackbird. Huck scurried to town, cashed in his gold, and bought equipment to lay a track into his mine.

Over the next few months, Huck continued to hit gold. In fact, he hit so much gold that his one car on his one track couldn't carry it all. The gold he dug began to collect in the back of the mine.

Other prospectors who'd heard about Huck's great find came by to see for themselves. They all tried to convince Huck to put more tracks in the mine. "If you do," they would say, "you can get all gold out faster. As it is, most of it is just sittin' there, deep in the mine."

Huck refused. No matter what others said to persuade him to lay more tracks, he just shook his head and walked away.

One day, a fellow by the name of Mark Twain stopped by; he too had heard about Huck's claim and wanted to satisfy his curiosity. He noticed a few other miners milling about and struck up a conversation with them.

"Seems that this fella's doin' pretty well," said Twain.

"Sure is," said the others.

"If he's doing so well," said Twain, "why doesn't he lay more tracks?"

"Mister," said one of the others, "you'll never convince him to do that."

"Why's that?" asked Twain.

"Because," replied the other, "Huck Finn's got a one track mine, and that's all there is to it."

See pages 99–102.

GOLDILOCKS

Sentence Combining

The following story is full is short sentences. Combine two or three at a time to create longer, more interesting sentences. You may need to add or delete words and change the tenses of some verbs.

It was the day after. The infamous "Bears Incident" had happened. Goldilocks was trying to return to life. She wanted a normal, quiet life. She found it impossible to do so. She was being hounded by reporters. Reporters hounded her constantly. Each reporter wanted to get an exclusive interview with her. Each reporter wanted to get her side of the story.

It was the end of the day. It was clear that the reporters were not going to leave her alone. They had set up camp on her front yard. No amount of pleading or prodding from her could get them to leave.

Goldilocks was reluctant. Goldilocks emerged from her house. Goldilocks faced the throng of reporters.

She started to utter a word. One reported shouted, "Miss Locks, rumor has it that you and the Bear Family have been at odds with one another for years. Is that true?"

Goldilocks replied, "Yes, it is true. The Bears and I do not get along."

Another reported asked, "What is the cause of the bad blood between you?"

Goldilocks answered, "Let's just say that for years we have not gotten along. Let's leave it at that."

A third reporter asked, "Why did you break into the Bears' house?"

Goldilocks replied, "I know that Mama and Papa Bear told Baby Bear to break my bicycle. I found it yesterday. I was mad. I knew I had to do something. I went to their house. I had three bears to cross."

GOLDILOCKS

Sentence Combining: Corrections

The day after the infamous "Bears Incident," Goldilocks was trying to return to a normal, quiet life. She found it impossible to do so because she was constantly being hounded by reporters, each wanting to get an exclusive interview with her, to get her side of the story.

By the end of the day, it was clear that the reporters were not going to leave her alone. They had set up camp on her front yard, and no amount of pleading or prodding from her could get them to leave.

Reluctantly, Goldilocks emerged from her house and faced the throng of reporters.

Before she could utter a word, one reported shouted, "Miss Locks, rumor has it that you and the Bear Family have been at odds with one another for years. Is that true?"

Goldilocks replied, "Yes, it is true that the Bears and I do not get along."

Another reported asked, "What is the cause of the bad blood between you?"

Goldilocks answered, "Let's just say that for years we have not gotten along and leave it at that."

A third reporter asked, "Why did you break into the Bears' house?"

Goldilocks replied, "I know that Mama and Papa Bear told Baby Bear to break my bicycle. And when I found it yesterday, I was so mad that I knew I had to do something. So I went to their house because I had three bears to cross."

See pages 103–105.

THE FROG PRINCE

More Sentence Combining

The following story is full is short sentences. Combine two or three at a time to create longer, more interesting sentences. You may need to add or delete words and change the tenses of some verbs.

The Frog Prince convened a gathering of frogs. These were all the frogs in his kingdom. The Frog Prince smiled. The Frog Prince surveyed the mass of amphibians. They were mumbling and talking. They were flipping and jumping. They were croaking and peeping.

The Frog Prince rose up to speak. A hush fell over the green gathering.

"My fellow frogs," said the Frog Prince, "you know, as well as I, that we are now facing grave danger. We are in danger from those rough skinned brutes, the Toads. For years now, the Toads have been encroaching on our lands; they have tried to invade our ponds; they have even attempted to steal our food."

The gathered frogs all croak. The frogs all peeped in agreement.

The Frog Prince continued, "As long as I am your leader, I pledge not to give in to the Toads' demands. We must stand firm. We must all come together. That means that Bullfrogs and Leopard Frogs and Tree Frogs and Peepers must put away your differences and come together in unity. . . ."

But the Frog Prince didn't get a chance to finish his sentence. He had been seized by a gigantic toad. The other frogs looked around. They found themselves surrounded by thousands of toads. They had no choice but to surrender.

They gave up. One frog said to another, "I never thought I'd live to see a *coup de toad*."

THE FROG PRINCE

More Sentence Combining: Corrections

After having convened a gathering of all the frogs in his kingdom, the Frog Prince smiled as he surveyed the mass of amphibians. They were mumbling and talking, flipping and jumping, and croaking and peeping.

The Frog Prince rose up to speak. A hush fell over the green gathering.

"My fellow frogs," said the Frog Prince, "you know, as well as I, that we are now facing grave danger from those rough skinned brutes, the Toads. For years now, the Toads have been encroaching on our lands; they have tried to invade our ponds; they have even attempted to steal our food."

The gathered frogs all croaked and peeped in agreement.

The Frog Prince continued, "As long as I am your leader, I pledge not to give in to the Toads' demands. We must stand firm. We must all come together. That means that Bullfrogs and Leopard Frogs and Tree Frogs and Peepers must put away your differences and come together in unity. . . ."

But the Frog Prince didn't get a chance to finish his sentence. He had been seized by a gigantic toad. When the other frogs looked around, they found themselves surrounded by thousands of toads. They had no choice but to surrender.

As they were giving up, one frog said to another, "I never thought I'd live to see a *coup de toad*."

See pages 103–105.

THE PRIZE

Sentence Sequencing

In the following story, the sentences are out of sequence. Put them in the "proper" sequence.

"Oh my!" cried his mother.

Jack's mother fretted.

Jack, who was holding three large bags, put them down.

She paced the kitchen and looked out the window each time she passed it.

He opened one of them and took out a harp. "This plays magical music," he said.

Jack replied quietly, "Mother, this hen lays golden eggs. It is my sleeping booty."

She said to Jack, "What is that?"

No matter what she did, though, she could not keep from worrying.

Jack opened the third bag and looked inside. He put his fingers to his lips and said, "Shh."

"Oh, Jack," cried his mother, "where have you been?"

"What did you find?" asked his mother.

"Oh my," said his mother.

He opened the second bag and took out handfuls of gold coins.

She tried to distract herself by cleaning, by knitting, by working on a jigsaw puzzle.

His mother looked inside the bag and saw a hen that was sleeping.

Then, the door opened and in walked Jack.

"Mother," exclaimed Jack, "I've been to the cloud-world, the one atop the giant beanstalk. You'll never guess what I found!"

She sat.

"These are for you, Mother," he said.

THE PRIZE

Sentence Sequencing: Corrections

Jack's mother fretted. She paced the kitchen and looked out the window each time she passed it. She sat. She tried to distract herself by cleaning, by knitting, by working on a jigsaw puzzle.

No matter what she did, though, she could not keep from worrying.

Then, the door opened and in walked Jack. "Oh, Jack," cried his mother, "where have you been?"

"Mother," exclaimed Jack, "I've been to the cloud-world, the one atop the giant beanstalk. You'll never guess what I found!"

"What did you find?" asked his mother.

Jack, who was holding three large bags, put them down. He opened one of them and took out a harp. "This plays magical music," he said.

"Oh my," said his mother.

He opened the second bag and took out handfulls of gold coins. "These are for you, Mother," he said.

"Oh my!" cried his mother.

Jack opened the third bag and looked inside. He put his fingers to his lips and said, "Shh."

His mother looked inside the bag and saw a hen that was sleeping. She said to Jack, "What is that?"

Jack replied quietly, "Mother, this hen lays golden eggs. It is my sleeping booty."

DO CHICKENS DANCE?

More Sentence Sequencing

In the following story, the sentences are out of sequence. Put them in the "proper" sequence.

The hall was filled with their happy clucks and squawks of amazement.

To celebrate, she decided to host the biggest ball any of her chicken friends had ever seen.

On Sunday the 15th, she was surprised to discover that the sky was still there.

There were chickens of every shape and size: fat chickens, thin chickens, tall chickens, short chickens, sharp-beaked chickens, flat-beaked chickens; there were chickens wearing rings, chickens wearing bows, chickens wearing glasses, chickens wearing hats; chickens in tights, chickens in wigs, chickens in sandles, chickens in boots.

Even though she was embarrassed about her proclamation, she was overjoyed that she had been wrong.

The headline of the story read: "Chicken Little's Fowl Ball Is Big Hit."

She sent out 4 boxcar loads of invitations, booked the biggest dance hall in the land, arranged to have a 50-piece orchestra to play from 6:00 until midnight, ordered 3 truckloads of refreshments, and bought enough party favors so that all who attended would be able to take something home.

In fact, Chicken Little's celebration was so big and such a huge success that it made front-page news in the local newspaper, *The Daily Cluck*.

On Saturday the 14th, Chicken Little proclaimed that the sky was falling.

On the night of the grand event, thousands and thousands of chickens arrived.

DO CHICKENS DANCE?

More Sentence Sequencing: Corrections

On Saturday the 14th, Chicken Little proclaimed that the sky was falling. On Sunday the 15th, she was surprised to discover that the sky was still there.

Even though she was embarrassed about her proclamation, she was overjoyed that she had been wrong. To celebrate, she decided to host the biggest ball any of her chicken friends had ever seen.

She sent out 4 boxcar loads of invitations, booked the biggest dance hall in the land, arranged to have a 50-piece orchestra to play from 6:00 until midnight, ordered 3 truckloads of refreshments, and bought enough party favors so that all who attended would be able to take something home.

On the night of the grand event, thousands and thousands of chickens arrived. The hall was filled with their happy clucks and squawks of amazement. There were chickens of every shape and size: fat chickens, thin chickens, tall chickens, short chickens, sharp-beaked chickens, flat-beaked chickens; there were chickens wearing rings, chickens wearing bows, chickens wearing glasses, chickens wearing hats; chickens in tights, chickens in wigs, chickens in sandles, chickens in boots.

In fact, Chicken Little's celebration was so big and such a huge success that it made front-page news in the local newspaper, *The Daily Cluck*. The headline of the story read: "Chicken Little's Fowl Ball Is Big Hit."

MUMMY'S THE WORD

Sentence Scramble

The sentences in following story are in the correct sequence, but each sentence is "scrambled"—its phrases and clauses are not in the correct order. Unscramble each sentence (capital letters that begin sentences and periods and other end punctuation have been deleted).

---

that of "mummy wrapper" in ancient Egypt and one of the most sought-after was one of most prestigious jobs

but they were well paid they also were greatly respected by Egyptians of every rank and office not only did these "wrappers" find special favor with the Pharaoh

a mummy wrapper not everyone could be

few were chosen in fact though many applied

to become painful and strict training a mummy wrapper required years of difficult

the ordeal of training the right touch survived and only those with the right spirit and

buried with the Pharaoh these mummy wrappers became they were sometimes and their names were inscribed in hieroglyphics so esteemed by the Egyptians that on a stone door in the tomb

was found in the tomb of King Tut the one thought to be the very first one mummy wrapper

and deciphered the etchings on the door when Egyptologists found "Here lies Achmed, the First Wrap Artist" the mummy wrapper's grave they were surprised to read

MUMMY'S THE WORD

Sentence Scramble: Corrections

In ancient Egypt, one of most prestigious jobs, and one of the most sought-after, was that of "mummy wrapper." Not only did these "wrappers" find special favor with the Pharaoh, but they were well paid; they also were greatly respected by Egyptians of every rank and office.

Not everyone could be a mummy wrapper. In fact, though many applied, few were chosen. To become a mummy wrapper required years of difficult, painful, and strict training. And only those with the right spirit and the right touch survived the ordeal of training.

These mummy wrappers became so esteemed by the Egyptians that they were sometimes buried with the Pharaoh and their names were inscribed in hieroglyphics on a stone door in the tomb.

One mummy wrapper, the one thought to be the very first, was found in the tomb of King Tut. When Egyptologists found the mummy wrapper's grave and deciphered the etchings on the door, they were surprised to read, "Here lies Achmed, the First Wrap Artist."

CRASH COURSE

Prepositional Phrases in the Wrong Places

The prepositional phrases in some of the following sentences are in the wrong places. Can you correct them?

The peace from another county was ruptured the day two wild Hobbits of the Shire burst onto the scene. At first, they were nothing but a distant rumble. As they got closer the rumble became a growl, and into the Shire as they blasted, the growl became a roar—a roar of engines.

Driving two hot-rods of the Shire, the Hobbits zoomed up and down the streets. They whipped ignoring stop signs and stoplights around corners. They gunned their engines and sent clouds into the air of exhaust billowing. Accelerating like rockets, of tire marks they left the scars in their wake.

Round and round the Shire they went. Faster and faster, fiercer and fiercer. It was clear that the Hobbit hot-rodders had no intention of stopping.

The mayor called the police chief and reported the Hobbits' wild and dangerous driving of the Shire.

"You've got to do something," said the mayor.

"I've already dispatched two patrol cars," said the police chief.

"I think you'll need more than two," said the mayor.

"Why?" asked the police chief.

"Well," said the mayor, "we've got to make them stop. You've got to get them to stop!"

"That will be difficult," said the police chief.

"Why?" asked the mayor.

"Because," said the police chief, "bad Hobbits almost never brake."

CRASH COURSE

Prepositional Phrases in the Wrong Places: Corrections

The peace of the Shire was ruptured the day two wild Hobbits from another county burst onto the scene. At first, they were nothing but a distant rumble. As they got closer the rumble became a growl, and as they blasted into the Shire, the growl became a roar—a roar of engines.

Driving two hot-rods, the Hobbits zoomed up and down the streets of the Shire. They whipped around corners, ignoring stop signs and stoplights. They gunned their engines and sent clouds of exhaust billowing into the air. Accelerating like rockets, they left the scars of tire marks in their wake.

Round and round the Shire they went. Faster and faster, fiercer and fiercer. It was clear that the Hobbit hot-rodders had no intention of stopping.

The mayor of the Shire called the police chief and reported the Hobbits' wild and dangerous driving.

"You've got to do something," said the mayor.

"I've already dispatched two patrol cars," said the police chief.

"I think you'll need more than two," said the mayor.

"Why?" asked the police chief.

"Well," said the mayor, "we've got to make them stop. You've got to get them to stop!"

"That will be difficult," said the police chief.

"Why?" asked the mayor.

"Because," said the police chief, "bad Hobbits almost never brake."

RENOVATION

Paragraph Sequencing

The paragraphs in the following story are out of sequence. Put them in their "proper" sequence.

One spring morning, the inhabitants of March Street were awakened by the sounds of pick and shovel, sledge and wheelbarrow, and grunting and straining. A small crowd gathered and observed a crew of workers dismantling and removing the last standing skeletal structures, now overgrown with weeds, of the House of Usher.

He took a breath and continued, "It is the Ides! It is the Ides! Beware the Ides of March!"

The residents of March Street convened an emergency meeting, trying to decide what to do about the grotesque replacement of the House of Usher. Ideas and counter-ideas were bandied about, but no one could arrive at a solution.

"Tell us!" came the reply.

No one on March Street knew, however, who had commissoned the razing of Usher and the building of a new house. Try as they might, the residents of March Street could not ferret out the name of the new owner. And with each passing day, the residents grew anxious.

"I know who owns the newly constructed house!" said the vice president.

As spring melted into summer, the work continued. Not only did the workers remove the remnants of the House of Usher, but they began building a new house upon the foundations of the old.

"My friends," said the vice president, "you thought that the Ushers were strange and mysterious, but they are nothing compared to the new residents of 221 March Street."

At midnight, the door of the meeting room burst open and in dashed the vice-president of the neighborhood association. "I have news!" he cried.

The new house, once it was completed in late August, took on a hideous aspect. The front of the house resembled nothing if not a distended, misshapen face, a face in the throes of agony. The windows of the place were oblong, like the eyes of a creature who lives in the nightmare territory of dreams. The paint of the house was blood-red, and even though it was dry, it carried a sheen that gave it a look of being perpetually wet.

"What news?" exclaimed the others.

After the House of Usher, on 221 March Street, collapsed, no one ventured near the rubble and ruins for years. As the years passed, the Ushers and their house were largely forgotten, and peace once again settled on the hedge-lined March Street.

RENOVATION

Paragraph Sequencing: Corrections

After the House of Usher, on 221 March Street, collapsed, no one ventured near the rubble and ruins for years. As the years passed, the Ushers and their house were largely forgotten, and peace once again settled on the hedge-lined March Street.

One spring morning, the inhabitants of March Street were awakened by the sounds of pick and shovel, sledge and wheelbarrow, and grunting and straining. A small crowd gathered and observed a crew of workers dismantling and removing the last standing skeletal structures, now overgrown with weeds, of the House of Usher.

As spring melted into summer, the work continued. Not only did the workers remove the remnants of the House of Usher, but they began building a new house upon the foundations of the old.

No one on March Street knew, however, who had commissoned the razing of Usher and the building of a new house. Try as they might, the residents of March Street could not ferret out the name of the new owner. And with each passing day, the residents grew anxious.

The new house, once it was completed in late August, took on a hideous aspect. The front of the house resembled nothing if not a distended, misshapen face, a face in the throes of agony. The windows of the place were oblong, like the eyes of a creature who lives in the nightmare territory of dreams. The paint of the house was blood-red, and even though it was dry, it carried a sheen that gave it a look of being perpetually wet.

The residents of March Street convened an emergency meeting, trying to decide what to do about the grotesque replacement of the House of Usher. Ideas and counter-ideas were bandied about, but no one could arrive at a solution.

At midnight, the door of the meeting room burst open and in dashed the vice-president of the neighborhood association. "I have news!" he cried.

"What news?" exclaimed the others.

"I know who owns the newly constructed house!" said the vice president.

"Tell us!" came the reply.

"My friends," said the vice president, "you thought that the Ushers were strange and mysterious, but they are nothing compared to the new residents of 221 March Street."

He took a breath and continued, "It is the Ides! It is the Ides! Beware the Ides of March!"

ANSWER KEY

Words the Spell-Check Won't Catch, page 2

aloud—audible
allowed—permitted

bear—animal
bare—without covering

awl—tool
all—everything

chili—hot pepper
chilly—cold

boarder—one who boards
border—boundary

weighted—heavy
waited—lingered

disbursed—paid out
dispersed—scattered

feet—plural of foot
feat—remarkable deed

idol—god
idle—lazy

caste—social class
cast—throw

yews—shrubs
ewes—lambs

chaste—modest
chased—ran after

aweigh—clear anchor
away—gone

dye—color
die—expire

meet—greet
meat—beef

Confusing Words, page 4

Correct Usage	Incorrect Usage
command—an order	commend—to praise
accepted—agreed	excepted—leave out
confidently—certainly	confidentially—privately
proceed—to begin	precede—to go before
imminent—impending	eminent—well known
apprise—to inform	appraise—to set a value
quite—very	quiet—not noisy
disapproved—withhold approval	disprove—prove false

More Confusing Words, page 6

Correct Usage	Incorrect Usage
desert—dry, barren region	dessert—sweet course at the end of the meal
recent—not long ago	resent—feel indignant
perfect—blameless	prefect—official
voracious—greedy	veracious—truthful
area—surface	aria—melody
through—beginning to end	thorough—complete
confident—sure	confidant—advisor
discomfit—to defeat	discomfort—uneasiness
descent—way down	decent—proper
commanded—ordered	commended—praised
dispersed—scattered	disbursed—paid out
accept—to agree	except—to leave out
bizarre—odd	bazaar—market

Homophones, page 8

flour should be flower
mist should be midst
would should be wood
Deer should be Dear
hare should be hair
plates should be plaits
lose should be loose
four should be for
past should be passed
board should be bored
herd should be heard
rode should be road
hare in the last sentence is correct because it refers to the rabbit

More Homophones, page 10

band—musical group
banned—forbidden

sight—a remarkable view
cite—to quote a passage

bases—plural of base
basis—foundation

bred—cultivated
bread—food

bate—to decrease
bait—to lure

hostel—shelter
hostile—unfriendly

brood—flock
brewed—steeped

bard—poet
barred—having bars

assistants—those who help
assistance—help

boulder—large rock
bolder—brave

allowed—permittted
aloud—audible

bettor—one who bets
better—superior

Filler Words, page 12

Filler words to be deleted: like, you know, so, goes

Spelling, page 18

If a word ends in a consonant, double the consonant before adding -ed or -ing.
Remember the rule: I before E except after C. (Leisurely is an exception to the rule.)

More Spelling, page 20

If a word ends in E, drop the E before adding -ing.
A lot is not one word.
Note that *calendar* ends in AR not ER.
Follow the rule: I before E except after C.

More Spelling, page 22

For words that end in E or a consonant, add -ly
For words that end in E, drop the E before adding -ing.
For single syllable words that end in a consonant preceded by a vowel, double the consonant before before adding -ed or -ing.

Punctuation, page 38

An apostrophe is needed to show possession. Example: *whale's*
Use a comma to separate a compound sentence connected with the word *and*.

Use commas to separate words in a series. Example: *hat, raft, and suspenders*

A direct quotation must be enclosed in double quotation marks.

An apostrophe is needed to show missing letters in a contraction. Example: *wasn't*

Complete sentences are separated with a period and each begins with a capital letter.

Clauses, phrases, and initial words like *yes, no,* and *oh* are separated by a comma.

If a name is used to address someone (example: *Oh, Captain Scree,*) the name is set off with a comma.

A quote within a quote is set off with single quotation marks. Example: *"I was always the first to say, 'Here I am.'"*

More Punctuation, page 40

An apostrophe is needed to show possession. Example: *Dorothy's*

Use a comma to separate a compound sentence.

A direct quotation must be enclosed in double quotation marks.

Use commas to set off a form of address. Example: *Oh, Captain Scree,*

An apostrophe is needed to show missing letters in a contraction. Example: *don't*

Use commas to set off an appositive. Example: *Glinda, the Good Witch of the North*

Complete sentences are separated with a period and each begins with a capital letter.

A question mark at the end of a quotation must be inside the quotation marks.

Capitalization, page 46

Capitalize the first word of a sentence.

Capitalize the first word of a direct quotation.

Capitalize proper nouns.

Capitalize the pronoun I.

Do not capitalize titles (captain, mother, president, etc.) unless followed by a name.

VERBS are words that refer to actions or states of being.

Verbs appear in six different forms, or tenses:

Present tense: Prufrock complains.

Past tense: Prufrock complained.

Future tense: Prufrock will complain.

Present perfect tense: Prufrock has complained ten times today.

Past perfect tense: Prufrock will have complained four times before lunch.

Future perfect tense: Prufrock will have complained more than 100 times by next Sunday.

In active voice the subject of the sentence—the person, animal, or thing performing the action—is present before the verb. "Man bites dog" is active voice.

In passive voice the subject of the sentence is usually not present. If the subject of the sentence is present it is often at the end of a prepositional phrase (it is the object of a preposition). "The man was bitten by the dog" is passive voice.

PRONOUNS come in three flavors, or cases: subjective, objective, and possessive. Subjective pronouns appear as "subjects" of sentences and phrases. Objective pronouns appear as "objects" of sentences, phrases, and clauses. Possessive pronouns show ownership of a noun.

There are also different kinds of pronouns:

Reflexive Pronouns refer to themselves: myself, yourself, himself, herself, itself, ourselves, yourselves, themselves

Demonstrative Pronouns indicate specific persons, places, or things: this, that, these, those

Indefinite Pronouns point to, generally not specifically, persons, places, or things: all, any, anyone, both, either, everybody, everyone, few, many, most, neither, nobody, none, several, some, somebody, someone

Relative Pronouns introduce clauses: which, who, whom, whose, that

Interrogative Pronouns introduce questions: what, which, who, whom, whose

PREPOSITIONS are words that tell how nouns and pronouns relate to other words in a sentence or other parts of a sentence.

Here is a list of commonly used prepositions:

about	below	for	throughout
above	beneath	from	to
across	beside	in	toward
after	besides	into	under
against	between	like	underneath
along	beyond	of	until
amid	but ("except")	off	unto
among	by	on	up
around	concerning	over	upon
at	down	past	with
before	during	since	within
behind	except	through	without

A group of words may act as a preposition:

on account of	in spite of
along with	together with

A preposition usually introduces a phrase. The noun or pronoun (plus other words like adjectives) that follows the preposition is called "the object."

Some prepositions tell when: during, till, before, since, about, after, through, for

Some prepositions tell which: with

Some prepositions tell what: into

Some prepositions tell where: above, across, around, behind, below, beside, next, in, underneath

Some prepositions compare things: like, as

CONJUNCTIONS are words that join words or groups of words. Some conjunctions, called coordinating conjunctions, link words or independent clauses: and, or, but, not, for, yet, so

Other conjunctions are called subordinating conjunctions; they introduce clauses. Here are some subordinating conjunctions that (usually) introduce adverbial clauses:

time	after, as, before, since, until, when, whenever, while, till
cause/reason	as, because, since, whereas, where
purpose/result	that, in order that, so that, provided, inasmuch as, as much as, if
condition	although, even though, unless, if, provided that, while, though, how

Another kind of conjunction is called a correlative conjunction. Correlative conjunctions always are seen in pairs. Here are some common pairs of correlative conjunctions:

both . . . and   either . . . or   neither . . . nor   not only . . . but also   whether . . . or

CAPITALIZATION & PUNCTUATION GUIDELINES

Capitalization

Capitalize these words:

 The first word of a sentence

 Names of the days of the week, months of the year

 The pronoun I

 Names, including initials, of individuals

 Titles that precede names

 All names of holidays (excluding any prepositions)

 The first word and all nouns in a salutation

 The first word in the complimentary closing of a letter

 Family relationship names when they precede a name or are used in place of person's name, especially in direct address

 All words in the names of specific organizations and agencies excluding prepositions, conjunctions, and articles

 Names of languages

 Names of definite sections of a country or the world

 Names of nationalities

 Names of religions and deities

 Adjectives formed from names of geographical locations, languages, races, nationalities, and religions

 The first word and all the words in titles of books, articles, works of art, etc., excluding short prepositions, conjunctions, and articles

Common Comma Uses

1. To separate two or more adjectives before a noun:
   The clear, shiny, polished mirror shattered.
2. To separate words or groups of words in a series:
   Puffing up his chin, squatting on the lily pad, and gazing at the moon, the bullfrog dreamed of flies.
   The hummingbird zipped through the open gate, past the willow tree, and into the forest.

3. To separate opening phrases in sentences:

   After a witnessing the destructive power of Frankenstein's creature, the crowd erupted with anger.

   Singing like a lark, the opera diva enthralled the audience.

4. To separate a phrase that interrupts the main thought in a sentence:

   The raven was, in the poet's opinion, an eerie and ominous bird.

   Ahab, the sea captain driven by the need for vengeance, hated his peg leg.

5. To separate an appositive phrase:

   Ebenezer Scrooge, the banker, was a stingy fellow.

   Brutus, the tragic hero in a famous play by Shakespeare, tried to do the right thing.

6. To separate two complete sentences with a connecting word (conjunction):

   Dorothy could have flown home with the Wizard in his balloon, or she could have booked a first class flight with a major airline.

   J. Alfred Prufrock tried to be heroic, but he was unsuccessful.

   George wanted to earn money, and he wanted to buy a farm.

7. To introduce a quotation in a sentence:

   One question that Prufrock asked himself was, "Do I dare to eat a peach?"

   Mark Antony repeatedly said, "Brutus is an honorable man!"

8. To separate the day from the year in a date:

   October 31, 2005

9. To separate a city from a state:

   Pocatello, Idaho

   Las Cruces, New Mexico

10. To separate a person's name and title:

    John Smythe, Director of Public Affairs

    Chief of Police, Cynthia Jones

11. To introduce a personal letter:

    Dear Long John Silver,

12. To separate a noun in a direct address:

    "Look, Rat!"

    "Stop, thief!"

    "Homer, look out!"

Common Apostrophe Uses

1. To show contractions:

   would not = wouldn't

   is not = isn't

it is = it's

will not = won't

2. To show that something belongs to someone:

Young Goodman Brown's bad luck

the pirate's hook

3. To show that something belongs to more than one person:

the doctors' offices

the deer's salt licks

Common Colon Uses

1. To introduce a list:

Sam Feathers disliked many things: new technology, hunters from the city, close-minded people, and the encroachment of subdivisions.

2. To introduce a business letter:

Dear Director:

Dear Sir:

Common Exclamation Point Use

To show strong emotion (surprise, excitement, anger, fear, etc.):

Oh yes!

The queen said, "Let them eat cake!"

Common Quotation Mark Use

To show who is speaking:

"Where are you?" bemoned Ishmael.

"I don't like the looks of this sky," said said the old man to his listeners, "but I'll continue until it rains."

Note that punctuation at the end of a direct quotation must be inside the quotation marks.

Common Semicolon Use

To join two independent clauses:

The old man wanted to bring the marlin back to shore; the sharks had other ideas.

The man had painted his face red and black; Robin looked at him and trembled.

Special Focus: The Comma Splice

When a comma is used in place of a semicolon, it is called a "comma splice." A comma splice is an incorrect way to use a comma; it is a usage error. A semicolon must connect two independent clauses; a comma cannot.

Here are examples:

Splice: Odysseus searched for a way home, Telemachus searched for Odysseus.

No Splice: Odysseus searched for a way home; Telemachus searched for Odysseus.

Splice: The crew was wide-eyed, they stood in amazement as the white whale breached.

No Splice: The crew was wide-eyed; they stood in amazement as the white whale breached.

Common Hyphen Uses

1. When spelled out, numbers greater than twenty-one contain a hyphen to join the elements, for example *thirty-three,* and *one-hundred-ninety-nine.*

2. To use with prefixes ex-, self-, all-; with prefixes before all proper nouns and adjectives; and with the suffix -elect:

    ex-president   president-elect   self-deception

3. To separate compound words when they operate as adjectives before a noun:

    a well-designed strategy   a well-rendered portrait

Common Dash Uses

1. To show a sudden shift in thought:

    Hopfrog opened his mouth—and here's where the story get's weird—and began to sing an aria.

2. To separate words that normally might appear in parentheses:

    Few ultramodern stories—roughly seven in number—have traditional plots.

3. To indicate such ideas as namely, in other words, that is, etc.:

    Captain Hook sought out Peter Pan for only one reason—revenge.

WHAT IS A SENTENCE?

A sentence is a group of words that express a complete thought. For this group of words to express a complete thought, it must have both a subject and a predicate. The subject is the word or words that are the main topic of the sentence; the predicate is the word or words that tell what the subject is doing or what condition the subject is in.

Every sentence must begin with a capital letter and end with a period, question mark, or exclamation point.

Each of the following is NOT a sentence:

> Jake
>
> Jake fishing in Michigan
>
> Ishmael and Ahab
>
> Ishmael and Ahab on the ship

Each of the following is a sentence:

> Jake sat down, took out a map, and began to make a plan.
>
> Jake loved fishing in Michigan.
>
> Ishmael and Ahab were destined to clash.
>
> Ishmael and Ahab both stood on the ship and mused about fate.

Parts of a Sentence:

Sentence Subjects: The subject is the topic of the sentence. The subject may be a word, a phrase, or a clause. In the following sentences the *subjects* are in italics.

> *John* is scaling the mountain. (single noun)
>
> *Scaling mountains* is John's passion. (gerund phrase)
>
> *The fellow scaling the mountain* is John. (noun + participial phrase)
>
> *The door* flew open. (article + noun)
>
> *To search for the white whale* was Ahab's quest. (infinitive phrase)
>
> *His rough, misshappen, bony fingers* reached for the key. (adjectives + noun)
>
> *That Ishmael needed a new line of work* is clear. (noun clause)

Sentence Predicates: The predicate tells what the subject is doing or what condition it is in. The predicate may be a word or a group of words. In the following sentences the *predicates* are in italics.

John *is scaling* the mountain. (linking verb + participle)

The fish *laughed* at the scuba diver.

Compound Subjects and Predicates

Both subjects and predicates can be compounds; that means that more than one of each of them can appear in a sentence. If a sentence has a compound subject it contains two or more subjects; the subjects are tied together by the words and, or, or nor. Compound subjects share the same verb (in the predicate).

The following sentences contain *compound subjects.*

Jack and Neil were hitchhiking to California. (nouns)

Either Emily Rose or Lady Jane stole the new shoes. (nouns)

Writing scary stories and talking to ravens are two of Edgar Allen Poe's favorite things. (gerund phrases)

The storm's rage and its fury lasted for nine days. (possessive noun & possessive pronoun)

To eat a peach and to wear his trousers rolled were two things that Prufrock wanted most in life. (infinitive phrases)

If a sentence has a *compound predicate* it contains two or more main verbs; the predicates are tied together by the words and, or, or nor. Compound predicates share the same subject.

The following sentences contain *compound predicates.*

Hawk Eye *ran* through the forest and *escaped* from his enemies. (verbs & prepositional phrases)

Dracula *opened* the coffin and *grabbed* a single rose. (verbs and direct objects)

Direct Object

A direct object is a word or group of words that follows a verb and answers the question what? or whom?

Man bites *dog.* (noun)

Aylmer decided *to remove the birthmark.* (infinitive phrase)

Aylmer's wife thought *that removing the birthmark was not a good idea.* (noun phrase)

We found it. (pronoun)

Owls love flying. (gerund)

Indirect Object

An indirect object is a word or group of words that follows a verb and tells to or for whom or what.

The Misfit gave *the grandmother* a choice.

The Frog Prince asked *the Princess* a question.

The three ghosts showed *Scrooge* the true meaning of Christmas.

Predicate Noun

A predicate noun follows a linking verb; it gives information about or identifies the subject of the sentence.

Hamlet is a tragic *hero*.

His happiness was her *grief*.

Predicate Adjective

A predicate adjective follows a linking verb; it gives information about the subject of the sentence.

The termagant's words were *viscious*.

After his party, Alfred was *quiet*.

Because he set his sights on vengeance, Abab became *myopic*.

Note that normally predicate adjectives follow a linking verb: am, are, is, was, were, been, will be, has been, will have been, could be, would be. Predicate adjectives also follow look, hear, taste, smell, sound, and other verbs such as appear, seem, become, grown, prove, remain.

About the Authors

KEITH POLETTE is an Associate Professor of English and the Director of the English Education program at the University of Texas, El Paso. He is a well-known speaker and presenter and is the author of two textbooks from Allyn and Bacon and several books for young readers.

NANCY POLETTE is Keith Polette's mother and a well-known author, presenter and speaker who has written many books for Teacher Ideas Press and Libraries Unlimited.

DATE DUE			